THINKING ACTIVITIES
FOR BOOKS CHILDREN LOVE

THINKING ACTIVITIES
FOR BOOKS CHILDREN LOVE

A Whole Language Approach

CAROLYN MOHR

DOROTHY NIXON

SHIRLEY VICKERS

Illustrated by

Kenda R. Kirby

TEACHER IDEAS PRESS
A Division of
Libraries Unlimited, Inc.
Englewood, Colorado
1988

TEACHER IDEAS PRESS
A Division of
Libraries Unlimited, Inc.
P.O. Box 3988
Englewood, CO 80155-3988

Library of Congress Cataloging-in-Publication Data

Mohr, Carolyn.
    Thinking activities for books children love : a whole language
approach / Carolyn Mohr, Dorothy Nixon, Shirley Vickers ;
illustrated by Kenda R. Kirby.
        xv, 206 p. 22x28 cm.
        ISBN 0-87287-697-7
        1. Thought and thinking--Study and teaching (Elementary)
2. Children--Books and reading. 3. Reading (Elementary)--Language
experience approach.   I. Nixon, Dorothy.   II. Vickers, Shirley.
III. Title.
LB1590.3.M64   1988
372.6--dc19   88-39450
                                                    CIP

This book is bound with Type II nonwoven material that meets and exceeds National Association
of State Textbook Administrators' Type II nonwoven material specifications Class A through E.

Table of Contents

Preface

Books that children love can be the basis for a whole language curriculum. Children's natural language is a motivational vehicle for learning. When given the opportunity to explore possibilities of answering questions and participating in activities using higher level thinking skills, students move from the passive to the active role of learning. The most effective way to motivate children is to use the experiences, materials, and literature that they love. Consequently, the choice of books in this publication were selected by children. As compiled in *Children's Books— Awards and Prizes*, the choices are consistently read and loved by third to sixth graders.

The primary purpose of the guides is to provide questions that encourage higher level thinking skills. In a technological age, this in-depth thinking will be the major survival skill of our children.

Specific objectives are as follows:

1. to present an organized sequence of thinking activities for selected books

2. to provide examples of questions at different levels of thinking

3. to provide guides that are flexible for use in a number of ways: large group instruction, small group instruction, centers, independent study, and team reading.

Introduction

The reading guides in this publication can be used in a variety of instructional methods. Examples are given below.

Introduction of Thinking Skills through Literature. The creative problem-solving pages are designed to introduce analysis, synthesis, and evaluation to the student. The teacher introduces the problem-solving activity before the novel is read. After reading the novel, student and author's solutions are compared.

Cooperative Teams. Students are assigned to teams to read a literature book, answering discussion questions. A recorder and reporter are assigned to report to other teams. While the teacher facilitates, students share ideas and work together.

Partner Reading. Students read one of the fifteen books. Using the guides, the students take turns asking and discussing questions. Oral reading is also practiced.

Independent Study with Contracts. A student's progress in an independent study of one of the novels may be monitored through student/teacher contracts. This provides both with feedback as to the direction that the study is taking.

Centers. By using the literature guides in centers, the student will be stimulated by higher level thinking processes. The center approach emphasizes individualized instruction based on student interest.

Gifted Classes and/or Gifted Child in Regular Classroom. The use of materials that emphasize analysis, synthesis, and evaluation motivate gifted learners. The guides may be used in correlation with an ongoing unit, with oral reading, or in large and small group discussions.

Media. The fifteen guides can be used by the media specialist as a model for other books. In addition, activities involving literary analysis, synthesis through role play, and evaluation via video production are all especially adaptable to media centers.

Finding Solutions

The problem-solving activities are designed to introduce students to the books in the guide. A brief synopsis and a major problem from each book are presented on the following pages. After reading the book, compare the author and student solution.

First: In spaces 1-5, write five possible solutions to solve the problem of your choice.

Second: List the ways that you will judge your ideas in spaces A-E. For example, is your idea dangerous or expensive?

Third: Rate each idea by referring to the Idea Rating Scale.

Fourth: Add the points for each idea and enter the total in the space provided. Compare the total points to determine the best problem-solving idea.

IDEA RATING SCALE
Points: 1—Poor, 2—Below Average, 3—Average, 4—Good, 5—Very Good

Measures (to judge how good your solutions are).	Possible Solutions				
	1.	2.	3.	4.	5.
A.					
B.					
C.					
D.					
E.					
Total Points					

Adapted from Bob Eberle and Bob Standish, *CPS FOR KIDS* (East Aurora, N.Y.: D.O.K. Publishers, Inc., 1980), p. 97. Printed with permission of D.O.K. Publishers, East Aurora, N.Y.

Creative Problem Solving

1. Peter has a very talkative brother. He is expecting a new brother or sister. And he has to think of the possibility of moving to a new, strange place. What can he do to adjust to all of these changes?

   Superfudge, by Judy Blume. New York: E. P. Dutton & Company, Inc., 1980.

2. Peter Hatcher has a rather large problem housed in a small body, his little brother Farley Drexel Hatcher, commonly called Fudge. His life is confused by all the things his brother does such as ruin his school assignments, spread mashed potatoes on restaurant walls, and, worst of all, getting into his room and destroying everything. How can he get everyone to appreciate him more and keep his brother from being such a pest?

   Tales of a Fourth Grade Nothing, by Judy Blume. A Yearling Book: New York: Dell Publishing Company, Inc., 1972.

3. A Siamese cat, an old bull terrier, and a young Labrador retriever attempt to travel back home over three hundred miles of Canadian wilderness. They have been purely domestic animals never even attempting to hunt their own food. What will they have to do to be successful in reaching their destination safely?

   The Incredible Journey, by Sheila Burnford. New York: Bantam Book: Little, Brown & Company, 1977.

4. Harvey, Carlie, and Thomas J. are foster children. They feel that they will never find security in a foster home. They think that they will always feel like pinballs out of control. What can the children do to feel more productive and secure in their new foster home?

   The Pinballs, by Betsy Byars. New York: Harper & Row, 1977.

5. Sarah Ida is spending the summer with Aunt Claudia because she has been unruly and devious at home. During her first day in her aunt's home, she takes money from a neighbor child. How can Sarah Ida learn the value of friendship and money?

   Shoeshine Girl, by Clyde Robert Bulla. New York: Thomas Y. Crowell Company, 1977.

6. Keith wants to have the mouse Ralph for a friend and secretly wants to take him home. He knows his parents will not agree to such an arrangement. What should Keith do to keep the secret from his parents?

   The Mouse and the Motorcycle, by Beverly Cleary. New York: William Morrow & Company, 1965.

7. Ramona Quimby is a bright and spirited kindergartner. She wants to grow up to be like her sister, Beezus. Ramona, however, after many desperate attempts to get attention, is expelled from school. What should Ramona do to gain positive attention and to reestablish her relationship with her teacher and classmates?

   Ramona the Pest, by Beverly Cleary. New York: William Morrow & Company, 1968.

8. Fifth-grader Elsie Edwards wants to make friends in her new school. Upon entering the class, the grossly overweight Elsie is rejected by all of her classmates. She is also found guilty of stealing the students' lunch money. What should Elsie do to change the attitudes of her classmates?

   Nothing's Fair in Fifth Grade, by Barthe DeClements. New York: Scholastic, Inc., 1981.

9. Hobie and his classmates develop a plan to make the new substitute cry. Later, however, Hobie feels guilty. He wants to retain his classmates' friendships but help the substitute too. What should Hobie do?

   Thirteen Ways to Sink a Sub, by Jamie Gilson. New York: Lothrop Lee & Shepard Books, 1982.

10. Their ordinary family life was suddenly changed by the arrival of a black and white bunny with glistening red eyes and fangs in place of teeth. Soon afterwards, the strangest things started happening. Vegetables dry up and turn white. Bunnicula, the rabbit, is out of his cage yet the cage is still locked. How can they stop these strange happenings and get on with their lives?

    Bunnicula, by Deborah Howe and James Howe. New York: Avon Books, a division of Hearst Corporation, 1979.

11. Milo Crinkley decided all he wants in life is to be *perfect*. He finds a book at the library that will help him achieve this in just three days providing he can complete each lesson. How can Milo achieve what he wants and learn to be happier about himself?

    Be a Perfect Person in Just Three Days, by Stephen Manes. Boston: Clarion Books, Ticknor & Field: A Houghton Mifflin Company, 1982.

12. Fourteen-year-old Jay Berry Lee only dreams of owning a pony and gun. That is until he discovers a tree full of monkeys. Having escaped from a circus train, they are valuable. How can Jay Berry capture the monkeys alive and win the handsome reward?

    Summer of the Monkeys, by Wilson Rawls. New York: Doubleday & Company, 1976.

13. Four friends are involved in a bet. Their friendship is threatened because the loser must come up with fifty dollars. How can they keep the bet and still be friends? What should they do?

How to Eat Fried Worms, by Thomas Rockwell. New York: Franklin Watts, Inc., 1973.

14. Twelve-year-old Ned has a weight problem. It interferes with all aspects of his life. He wants to be thinner, but lacks the willpower to follow any weight reducing program. What should he do?

Jelly Belly, by Robert Kimmel Smith. New York: Delacorte Press, 1981.

15. Peter has his own room that is just perfect. Suddenly his grandfather comes to live with them and needs *his* room. He is moved upstairs to a dingy, gross room that even his friends can't stand. What could Peter do to get his old room back?

The War with Grandpa, by Robert Kimmell Smith. A Yearling Book: New York: Dell Publishing Company, Inc., 1984.

Superfudge
by
Judy Blume

Superfudge
by
Judy Blume

It is bad enough that twelve-year-old Peter has a young brother Fudge who is a pain, but he is getting a new sister or brother! It is enough to make Peter want to run away. On top of these hassles, the family plans to move to Princeton for a year.

In the move, Peter faces new surroundings. He must leave his best friend Jimmy Fargo and will have to attend the same school as Fudge. Fudge is a talking machine and very creative. He keeps everyone in the school and at home on their toes.

The new baby is a girl. Peter and Fudge experience the trials of having a new baby called Tootsie. This brings new responsibilities and takes away some of the attention from the boys. Peter's greatest fear is that Tootsie will grow into another Fudge.

Princeton is not so bad after Peter meets a new friend named Alex and Fudge gets a new pet. Fudge also meets a new friend whose name is Daniel.

Being in the same school as Fudge sometimes proves to be embarrassing to Peter, but he manages with the help of his friends.

Peter adjusts to Princeton but before the year is finished his parents agree to move back to New York. This makes for mixed feelings for Peter.

Everyone in the family grows in different ways in this humorous, realistic book.

Chapters 1 and 2

VOCABULARY:
  tousled
  duet
  privilege

KNOWLEDGE:
  1. How old is Fudge?
  2. What news does Peter hear from his parents that upsets him?
  3. Who is Sheila Tubman?
  4. Was the baby a girl or boy?

COMPREHENSION:
  1. Describe Peter's feelings toward Fudge.
  2. Restate the threat Peter gives his parents about what will happen if he doesn't like the baby.
  3. Report what Fudge does with the baby that frightens his mother.
  4. Identify the statement Sheila makes that bothers Peter.

APPLICATION:
  1. Interpret why Peter feels that "They're going to have another Fudge."
  2. Have you ever dreaded something that turned out okay? Share.
  3. Make a drawing of Peter's family.
  4. What makes you want to *run away* at times?

ANALYSIS:
  1. How did Fudge act in a different way than Peter to having a new brother or sister?
  2. Examine the items owned by Peter. Are they similar to yours?
  3. What parts of chapters 1 and 2 did you find funny?
  4. How is your family different from Peter's?

SYNTHESIS:
  1. Organize a skit showing the scene where Mother tells Peter and Fudge they are going to have a baby.
  2. What name would you give to a new baby girl?
  3. Pretend you are Fudge. Create a commercial to sell the baby.
  4. Remembering Peter's feelings about having a new baby, compose a birth announcement from his point of view.

EVALUATION:
  1. Decide some positive things that might come from having a new baby sister.
  2. Why do you think Fudge was acting like a baby?
  3. Do you think Peter's reaction concerning the new baby was fair to his parents?
  4. Do you think the size of Peter's ears is important? Why?

Chapters 3 and 4

VOCABULARY:

desperate	zillion
suspense	humid
leave of absence	contraption

KNOWLEDGE:
1. What made Peter's mother cry harder?
2. Where will the Hatcher family be moving?
3. Who is Turtle?
4. What did Fudge do to Tootsie?

COMPREHENSION:
1. Describe where the Hatchers live.
2. How will the house in Princeton be different from their apartment in New York?
3. How can Mr. Hatcher take the year off?
4. Why didn't Peter choose to stay the year with Jimmy?

APPLICATION:
1. Interpret why Peter and Jimmy became angry at each other about Peter's moving.
2. Draw a picture of Turtle.
3. Design an ad for renting a house for the Thatcher family.
4. How would you feel if you learned today that you would be moving to Princeton, New Jersey?

ANALYSIS:
1. Compare Peter's reaction to moving to learning about having a new baby in the family.
2. Describe the inside of Peter's apartment building and his family's apartment.
3. Analyze the meaning when Peter says to Fudge, "You're off the wall...."
4. Discover how far Princeton, New Jersey, is from where you live.
5. Compare Peter's feelings about Tootsie as he held her on his lap to his feelings of what she might be like before she was born.

SYNTHESIS:
1. Design a symbol that represents Fudge and Peter.
2. Prepare three feelings of "unfairness" Peter has toward his parents. Share with a classmate.
3. Organize a list of things you have that you would take in a carton of special things if you were moving.
4. Predict how Peter will react to his new home. Explain.

EVALUATION:
1. Judge what will be the most important changes in the Hatchers' lives due to the move.
2. Do you think Fudge is smart for a four-year-old? Why?
3. Decide why you think Peter did not throw the Kreskin's Crystal out of the window.
4. Did Peter do the right thing to "sic" Turtle on Sheila?

Chapters 5 and 6

VOCABULARY:

organically   phase

regenerate   personality conflict

allergic

KNOWLEDGE:

1. What is the new game Fudge is playing on Peter?
2. Who is Peter's new friend?
3. Why does Fudge kick his kindergarten teacher?
4. How do Peter and Fudge get to school the first day?

COMPREHENSION:

1. Describe Mom's reaction to the worms.
2. Explain the meaning of the chapter title "Small Ones Are Sweeter."
3. Report what Fudge did on his first day of kindergarten.
4. Describe the meaning of the chapter title "Farley Drexal Meets Rat Face."

APPLICATION:

1. Write an imaginative paragraph about something you might have done during the summer.
2. Have you ever been called to see the principal or someone that you were worried about seeing and tried to reason like Peter? Share your experience.
3. Draw a picture of the Thatchers' home in Princeton.
4. Calculate how many worms Peter and Alex would have the next time for Mrs. Muldour.

ANALYSIS:

1. Compare a time you could not sleep because like Peter in chapter 6 something new was going to happen to you.
2. Compare the house in New Jersey to the apartment in New York.
3. Discover what it means to be creative.
4. Analyze the projects Mr. Bogner plans for the sixth grade class. Do you predict Peter will like them?

SYNTHESIS:

1. Create a new name for an ice cream flavor.
2. Predict what Mrs. Muldour does with the worms.
3. Survey nicknames of class members.
4. Research facts about Princeton University.

EVALUATION:

1. Do you think Alex and Peter will become good friends?
2. Decide what feelings Peter was having during the first two weeks at Princeton.
3. Do you think Fudge was creative his first day of kindergarten?
4. What do you think Fudge will be like in Ms. Ziff's class?
5. Why do you think Fudge is afraid of monsters?

Chapters 7 and 8

VOCABULARY:

educational	Parlez-vous Français?
bonjour	fortified
snorted	exaggerate
coincidence	

KNOWLEDGE:
1. What did Fudge want to take to school for show and tell?
2. What did Fudge take to school for show and tell?
3. What does Mrs. Muldour have for Halloween treats?
4. What is Peter and Fudge's secret at the end of chapter 8?

COMPREHENSION:
1. Explain what is funny about Uncle Feather's conversation with Mrs. Hildebrant.
2. Describe what embarrassed Grandma.
3. What happens to Peter when Alex is dressed for Halloween?
4. Why is Jimmy's father's painting entitled "Anita's Anger?"

APPLICATION:
1. Draw a picture of Uncle Feather.
2. Interview classmates. Find out what "phases" they have experienced.
3. Have you ever had changes in your life that made everything different? Share your experiences.
4. Create a commercial for bird food.

ANALYSIS:
1. Analyze what Grandma means by "Everybody needs attention."
2. Compare Uncle Feather's talking to Fudge's game.
3. Analyze what it means when Peter's dad states, "And sometimes you've got to do what's really important to you, even when it's not practical."
4. Research the vitamins in popular cereals. Conclude what is *fortified*.

SYNTHESIS:
1. Imagine you could have a new pet. What would it be? What would be its name?
2. Create a new title for chapter 5.
3. Research what steps you must take to write an article or book.
4. Compare "Anita's Anger" to a Dr. Seuss book. Why is it thought both can be done in an hour?

EVALUATION:
1. Why do you think Fudge is no longer afraid of monsters and sleeps in his own room?
2. Are you a middle child? Decide why these children need attention.
3. How do you know Peter is homesick for New York in chapter 8?

4. Why do you think the author used "Naturally Fortified" for the title of chapter 8?
5. Do you think Dr. Seuss wrote his books in one hour?

Chapters 9 and 10

VOCABULARY:

pudgy	original
species	mimicked
conference	unanimous

KNOWLEDGE:
1. What has Tootsie learned that changes things in the Thatcher household?
2. Who is Fudge's friend?
3. Where did Fudge get the phrase "It is never too early."
4. What holiday does Daniel celebrate?

COMPREHENSION:
1. Describe Daniel.
2. What happened at the movies that caused the friends to tease Peter?
3. What were Peter's fears about Fudge being a genius?
4. Fudge is a "great pretender." What does this mean?

APPLICATION:
1. Draw a picture of Turtle imitating Tootsie.
2. List the characteristics of the myna bird that you have learned from Daniel.
3. Write a letter to Santa asking for something that does not cost money.
4. Give a gift certificate you have made that does not cost any money to someone.

ANALYSIS:
1. What parts of chapter 9 did you find funny or embarrassing?
2. Research the myna bird. Report your findings in a creative way of your choice.
3. Research different holiday customs and their origins. Why do we use mistletoe at Christmas time?
4. Why is chapter 9 entitled "Superfudge"?

SYNTHESIS:
1. Imagine you came from another planet. Describe your home.
2. Give an introduction to a classmate that is similar to Daniel's.
3. Create a new chapter title for chapter 10.
4. Plan a party for your school room.

EVALUATION:
1. Why do you think Peter did not feel good about Alex and Jimmy becoming friends?
2. Was Mom clever in getting rid of Daniel for supper? Explain.
3. Judge which character is the most imaginative.
4. Decide why Mom and Dad are so tired on Christmas day.

Chapters 11 and 12

VOCABULARY:

catastrophe	inconsiderate
aggressive	appropriate
toddling	rebus

KNOWLEDGE:
1. Who comes to visit the school?
2. What is Fudge's first catastrophe?
3. Recall Tootsie's first word.
4. What embarrassed Peter at the special program?

COMPREHENSION:
1. Describe the drawing made by the author who visited the school. Who is it?
2. Explain why Mr. Green said that Fudge would try harder for a catastrophe next time.
3. Describe the trick Fudge played on Peter.
4. Explain what Mr. Green means by "That's because I took a lot of chances."

APPLICATION:
1. What is wrong with Fudge jumping off his bike rather than using his brakes? Have you ever done this?
2. Explain the differences of Peter and Fudge's attitude toward the author.
3. Redraw the Hatcher family. Compare it to your first drawing.
4. How was Peter feeling when Fudge was gone? Relate a similar experience you have had.

ANALYSIS:
1. What three catastrophes made Mom's definition of catastrophe correct?
2. Discover what Dad figures out about his writing. Is he a failure?
3. Analyze the pun "There is no place like 'Nu Yuck.' "
4. Survey how many of your classmates would like to live in New York.

SYNTHESIS:
1. Create a drawing of someone. Have friends guess who it might be.
2. Imagine that you are having an author visit your school. Who would you want it to be?

3. Write a brief paragraph describing a humorous situation in your family.
4. Write a letter to an old friend telling him or her that you are moving back to your former home.

EVALUATION:
1. Why do you think Fudge is so outspoken?
2. What kind of a man is Mr. Green?
3. Decide what changes will be in store for the Thatcher family when they return to New York.
4. Why do you think it was "all worth it" to go back to New York?

Additional Activities

VISUAL ART:
1. Make an illustration book of the chapters in *Superfudge*.
2. Create a bookmark using an incident, character, or object from *Superfudge*.
3. Draw one of the characters and write a description that includes physical and personality characteristics.

DRAMA:
1. Create a commercial for one of the products in the book.
2. Dramatize a scene you thought particularly funny in the book.
3. Interview Mr. Green, the principal, on his thoughts about losing Fudge and Peter back to a school in New York.

CREATIVE WRITING:
1. Write a short essay about your family.
2. Secretly create a book cover and synopsis for *Superfudge*. Compare ideas with classmates.
3. Write a paragraph describing an incident when you were embarrassed by the actions of someone else.
4. Write a summary of *Superfudge* making an outline of the events.
5. Create a rebus of the book title *Superfudge*. Share with your classmates.
6. Rewrite the ending having the Hatcher family remain in Princeton.

SOCIAL STUDIES/SCIENCE:
1. Research differences in living in a large city and living in a rural community. Compare the advantages and disadvantages.
2. Research organic gardening.
3. Discuss the idea that life experiences are constantly changing but basic values remain the same. Relate experiences.
4. Have a geography lesson on the northeast. Contrast population, industry, and occupations.
5. Create family trees with adjectives describing various personalities.
6. Chart differences and hazards of your environment with that of the northeast.

Bulletin Board

1. Students prepare lists of victories experienced by characters in the book. These are pinned on the left side of the figure.

2. Individual student's victories are described in writing and are pinned on the right side of the figure.

3. Students' definitions of the concept *victory* are placed on the bulletin board.

Tales of a
Fourth Grade Nothing

by
Judy Blume

Tales of a
Fourth Grade Nothing

by
Judy Blume

This story centers around the Hatcher family who live in New York City near Central Park. They have two sons, Peter and an "almost" three-year-old nicknamed Fudge.

Peter tells the story from his point of view and most of it revolves around the misadventures of his brother, Fudge.

Fudge is one of those children who always seems to be touching the wrong thing or creating havoc wherever he goes. He is the bane of his brother's existence.

His excapades run from spreading mashed potatoes on restaurant walls to actually swallowing his brother's turtle.

It presents an interesting view of family involvement and adjustment to each other.

Chapters 1 and 2

VOCABULARY:

hide-a-bed   slurping
measly   insulted
babbling

KNOWLEDGE:
1. Where did Peter win his turtle as a prize?
2. What did he have to do to win it?
3. What name did he give it?
4. Explain why Peter's dad needs to watch so much television?
5. What is Peter's little brother's legal name? His nickname?
6. Tell one way Fudge will stay quiet for a time.
7. What did Fudge eat off the dining room table that was most unusual?
8. Name an advantage of being nine.

COMPREHENSION:
1. How much of a difference was there between Peter's guess and the actual number of jelly beans?
2. Explain what some of the limitations might be, in Peter's mind, about having a turtle as a pet.
3. Tell why Peter is so upset with his mother's interpretation of *scrub*.
4. Tell about Peter's biggest problem and why he considers it impossible to correct.

APPLICATION:
1. List possible choices for good turtle names.
2. Research information on the proper care of a turtle. If possible, get one as a class pet so the children can make daily observations.
3. Experiment with stamps. See how much residue is left on an item after they have been pulled off. Do you think cleaning the suitcase would have been difficult?

ANALYSIS:
1. Analyze why Peter felt the others would have preferred his turtle to the goldfish they had won.
2. Do you believe the Yarbys knew very much about children? Explain.
3. Explain if you feel Peter's frustration with Fudge is justified. Cite examples from either your own family or one you know.

SYNTHESIS:
1. Judy Blume is a very popular children's author with several books to her credit. Obtain copies of as many as you can and create an author's corner. Some items you might include: (1) research material about her life, (2) write letters to her in care of her publisher and keep copies in the corner.
2. Create a book banner for this story.
3. Write a dialogue between Mr. and Mrs. Yarby after they see their decorated suitcase.
4. Take the dialogue above and extend it to include their next conversation with Mr. and Mrs. Hatcher.

EVALUATION:
1. Discuss the term *sibling rivalry* and its involvement with this book.
2. Evaluate your feelings about your sisters or brothers. Also, consider what their feelings about you are. Are both accurate or biased? Explain.
3. Which character would you rather be—Peter or Fudge? Explain.
4. Judge whether or not you feel Mr. Hatcher deserved to lose the Yarby account over the misunderstanding.

Chapters 3 and 4

VOCABULARY:

commercial	tumbled
cocker spaniel	motioned
relieved	mugged
cooties	imitate
bowling	peroxide

KNOWLEDGE:
1. What did Fudge suddenly do that really upset his mother?
2. How did their mother get food into Fudge's mouth?
3. What was Peter's reaction to Fudge's punishment?
4. Why couldn't Fudge stand on his head?
5. What does Peter feel is the very worst thing about Sheila?
6. Explain why the trees don't experience the traditional fall foliage colors in New York City.
7. Why can Jimmy easily imitate different foreign accents?

COMPREHENSION:
1. Explain the family's attitude toward the loss of the Juicy-O account.
2. Describe the police procedure one goes through after a mugging.
3. How did his mother get Fudge to open his mouth?
4. Describe the events leading up to the accident.
5. Children's chase games often include the term *cooties*. Explain what this means and how it is played.

APPLICATION:
1. Draw your concept of the phrase "monkey business at meal times."
2. Do a report on Central Park including where it's located, how large an area it entails, and other interesting facts.
3. Describe Fudge. Use as many descriptive words as possible.
4. Using the same directions as above, describe Peter.
5. List various adjectives showing Peter's feelings towards his brother. Compare the lists compiled by each student. Which words are repeated most often?
6. Define the term *mugging*.

ANALYSIS:

1. Analyze your feelings regarding Mr. Hatcher's reaction to Fudge's behavior. Do you agree or disagree? Explain. Would your position change if you were Mr. Hatcher or Fudge?
2. Discuss the assumed attitude that sooner or later everyone living in New York City will be mugged.
3. Compare Fudge's behavior to that of other children his age. Organize a class discussion.
4. Explain whether after the accident Mrs. Hatcher's anger toward Peter was justified.

SYNTHESIS:

1. Fudge's favorite expression was "Eat it or wear it." Draw some examples of people doing just that with foods that would be interesting and distinctive to draw.
2. Use Peter's problem as a letter writing exercise. Have him write a letter to an advice columnist.
3. Have the students write a new ending for the flying adventure. In this one have Peter take more responsibility for Fudge.
4. Create a collage of pictures showing the foods you feel would have tempted Fudge to eat.
5. Draw Peter's fantasy about his real mother.

EVALUATION:

1. Fudge's accident was serious and potentially very dangerous. Evaluate why so many childhood accidents fall into this category.
2. Judge what potential problems could be created if Mrs. Hatcher continues to show preference between her sons.
3. "But never to me" was Peter's absolute statement regarding any future relationship between himself and Sheila. Select examples from your life where you have stated *never* or *always* and evaluate the final result.

Chapters 5 and 6

VOCABULARY:

fang	patience
racket	insult
vampire	untangled
behave	temper tantrum
rearrange	loafers

KNOWLEDGE:

1. Explain Peter's concept of Fudge's appearance without his teeth.
2. Relate the reason behind the nickname "fang."
3. What was so hard to believe about Jennie? Why did Peter think that of her?
4. Which present produced a violent reaction from Fudge?
5. Which child copied a natural behavior of Dribble?
6. Explain Peter's procedure of cleaning Dribble's home.
7. What excuse did the dentist give children so they would open their mouth?

COMPREHENSION:
1. Describe his mother's dislike of Fudge's new name.
2. Explain which one of the children was very sensitive. Give examples to support your opinion.
3. Tell which trick, used by Peter in an earlier chapter, helped solve the dentist's problem.
4. Recount Peter's decision regarding his brother after their outing.
5. Explain how Mrs. Hatcher tricked Fudge about his shoes.

APPLICATION:
1. List all of Fudge's embarrassing behaviors during the family outings.
2. Define the term *chip off the old block*. Survey the class to see when they have been called the same thing in their family. Record the answers.
3. Using a children's party book, choose a game suitable for three-year-olds. Experiment with it on your classmates.

ANALYSIS:
1. Analyze Peter's reasons for making the statement "My mind is my own." Relate that to times in your life when you have felt the same way.
2. Relate the reasons behind Fudge's temper tantrum. Would you have corrected him the same or differently than Mrs. Hatcher?
3. Interpret if Peter had any compassion for Fudge and his behavior.
4. Considering everyone involved in the movie incident, who would have been most

Chapters 7 and 8

VOCABULARY:

traffic congestion   monorail
chain latch   hailed
zoomed   arrangements

KNOWLEDGE:
1. Explain the reason the class was divided into their particular committees.
2. What was the topic given Peter's group?
3. State Sheila's feelings regarding the proper color for the poster board.
4. Tell why the boys didn't like the cover Sheila created.
5. Explain how the cover was altered so all committee members were pleased.
6. What was Fudge's new profession?
7. Why were so many mothers and children at the agency?
8. Recall the reason Sheila always carries the committee booklet.
9. What word did Peter hear his brother use for the first time?

COMPREHENSION:
1. What were the three areas of transportation they wanted to research?
2. Explain why Sheila was unhappy with their committee members.
3. Tell why Mrs. Hatcher doesn't believe in locks on a door.
4. Explain the accidental hiring for the commercial.
5. This section states the reason Peter refers to himself as a "fourth grade nothing." State his reasoning for this attitude.

APPLICATION:
1. Draw an illustration of how Fudge looked at the conclusion of chapter 8.
2. List the reasons Peter was happy to stay with his dad.
3. Sketch your concept of the poster they created. Use the given description as a basis.

ANALYSIS:
1. Analyze the positives and negatives of their working committee. Brainstorm how they can improve this relationship.
2. The author has explained the excessive pollution in New York and its effect on the trees. Equate this to its effect on people.
3. Summarize these two chapters in no more than two short paragraphs. Choose one incident you found most humorous or where you found your sympathy was strongly on Peter's side.

SYNTHESIS:
1. All of Fudge's behavior has been written from Peter's point of view. Rewrite one incident as if Fudge was writing the book.
2. Create your own poster depicting transportation. Refine their ideas into a more effective product.

3. Design a model of a monorail system. Explain its energy source, where it would run in relation to the ground, potential speed, and number of passengers it could accommodate at one time.
4. Create another new energy source which would reduce pollution in New York City. Be creative and use your imagination.

EVALUATION:
1. Who do you feel was smarter or more clever, Peter or Fudge? Or, do you feel, for a reason such as the age difference, it could be unfair to evaluate? Defend your position.
2. Explain why you believe Fudge is always getting into negative situations.
3. Evaluate Peter's statement that he wonders "how anyone would ever manage his brother without his help." Express your opinion.

Chapters 9 and 10

VOCABULARY:

ushers	kidnap
conclusion	omelet
squinted	gym
cradled	dreary

KNOWLEDGE:
1. Explain the occurrence in the movie that allowed Fudge to later slip off unnoticed.
2. Recall the first thing Peter noticed after school that led him to worry that something had happened in his room.
3. Where was Dribble?
4. How were they able to show Peter where his turtle was?
5. Explain what his parents gave him to replace Dribble.
6. What did Peter name him?

COMPREHENSION:

1. Explain Fudge's reason for leaving his movie seat.
2. Tell why Peter came up with still another *never* regarding Fudge.
3. Describe Peter's reaction to Dribble being missing. Why did he feel Fudge had to be involved?
4. Explain why Peter didn't like Fudge as much after the phone rang.
5. Summarize everyone's attitude and concern for Dribble.

APPLICATION:

1. List all of the problems Fudge managed to create before the end of the movie.
2. Draw a picture of Peter's reaction to sampling the omelet.
3. Role play the scene between Peter and Fudge where Fudge finally tells where Dribble is and why. Consider how Peter is feeling and why Fudge keeps smiling.
4. Remember playing "telephone" as a child? You all sit in a circle and the first person whispers a word to the person next to him or her until it travels the circle. The first person repeats the initial word as well as the resultant word. Compare this to the neighbors gossiping about Fudge and the turtle.

ANALYSIS:

1. Analyze why Peter's father wanted their activities of the past days to remain "kind of a man's secret."
2. Interpret if there isn't some logic in many of Fudge's responses.
3. Relate why Peter couldn't understand his mother's concern over Fudge. After all, *his turtle* was gone. Did the blankets help at all?
4. Analyze the subtle differences in why both Peter and his mother were upset at the turtle swallowing incident.

SYNTHESIS:

1. Draw a picture of the three of them walking down a New York street to the movie.
2. Imagine Fudge had really been lost. Create a lost-and-found advertisement. Be certain to include some unusual characteristics; ones that might aid in locating him.
3. Create the telephone conversation between Mother and the ambulance driver. Remember her frustration.

EVALUATION:

1. Have the students compare this to other Judy Blume books. Rate the ones you know in order of preference starting with your favorite. Discuss and defend your choices.
2. At the conclusion of several previous chapters, Peter and his mother would just laugh following Fudge's antics. This chapter saw Peter and his father doing the very same thing. Why is it, after getting everything straightened out, sometimes there isn't anything else to do *but* laugh? Relate a similar story from your life.

Additional Activities

ART:
1. Create a scrapbook of Fudge Behaviorisms. Illustrate each.
2. Design party decorations, favors, napkins, and a table centerpiece in a theme which reflects Fudge's age and uniqueness. Design a place mat for each guest which is distinctive of that particular person's personality.
3. Create a brand new birthstone for Fudge. Give it special qualities.

DRAMA:
1. Role play the scene in the restaurant. Have students play not only Mrs. Hatcher, Peter, and Fudge, but the waitress and other customers.
2. Create a mime of a shoe salesman trying shoes on different people. Examples might include a baby, old person, young child, teenager, mother with children, and harried businessman running late for an appointment. Have them guess the subject of each.
3. Develop a monologue for Fudge telling how he innocently gets into these situations. Remember your character is three years old — give him appropriate mannerisms and speech pattern.
4. Perform charades showing different activities of Fudge. Have the other students identify each event.

CREATIVE WRITING:
1. Personify the life of a turtle. Create a fantasy adventure for him. Keep in mind his size, etc., and how that would alter his perspective.
2. Write a script for the bike commercial. Either share and compare the various scripts creating a class version to videotape or have each group videotape their own.
3. Create a new adventure for Peter and Fudge. This time alter their roles and, subsequently, the outcome.

MUSIC:
1. Varied concerts have been held in Central Park, including Diana Ross and Simon and Garfunkel. Research the various artists, their differing styles, and types of music. Listen to either of these sound tracks or obtain the videos. Choose at least one song you feel was most effectively performed in that setting. Explain what would be some of the positive as well as the negative aspects of having such shows presented outside.

SCIENCE
1. Research and report on the life cycle of a turtle. Record the most interesting facts. Possible questions: (1) comparison between land and water turtles, (2) how one can tell their age, (3) means of protection, (4) food sources, and (5) life expectancy.
2. Write a minipaper on x-ray including its discovery as well as its special uses today. If possible, invite a radiologist to speak to the class about different aspects of his or her profession.
3. If anyone knows someone living in New York, have them send different leaf examples to compare to the same varieties from other locations.

SOCIAL STUDIES:

1. Draw an aerial view of Central Park marking the key points of interest. Research the historical reason for its existence.

2. Research other cities throughout the world having pollution and population problems similar to that of New York City. Compare and contrast the various areas as to similarities both in industry and economic base. What causes the pollution? Are any possible solutions being seriously considered?

3. Have students write to the tourist office and the chamber of commerce to gather material regarding New York City. Assign different well-known landmarks. Possible choices might be:

Statue of Liberty	Wall Street
Rockefeller Center	Guggenheim Museum
Metropolitan Museum of Art	Broadway
Greenwich Village	Empire State Building
Chinatown	Radio City Music Hall
American Museum of Natural History	

Bulletin Board

1. Have each student bring a baby picture.

2. Assign a secret pal to every child.

3. Have each student interview their subject outside of class to obtain biographical information including family, interests, pets, hobbies, future plans, etc.

4. You assign a number to each picture/information sheet and tack it on the bulletin board.

5. Each student then has a sheet with the corresponding numbers and sees how many classmates they can match with the correct number after hearing the information about each.

Crossword Puzzle

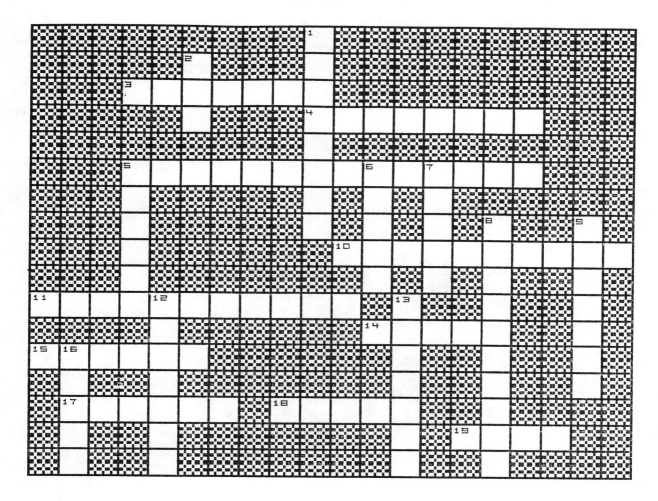

ACROSS CLUES

3. Fudge ate these, either petal by petal or all at once.
4. Where they took Fudge after Dribble disappeared.
5. The subject of Peter's school committee report.
10. Peter's gift from the Yarbys.
11. Mr. Hatcher's profession.
14. Farley Drexel Hatcher's nickname.
15. What Fudge put all over the Yarby's suitcase.
17. Place where Fudge got lost.
18. What Peter and his mother decided wasn't a good idea to have for three year olds.
19. Peter's nickname for Fudge that his mother forbade him to use.

DOWN CLUES

1. Dribble's home.
2. Peter's new pet.
5. The prize Peter won at Jimmy Fargo's birthday party.
6. Fudge's windup present.
7. What Fudge lost when he tried to *fly*.
8. Fudge's television debut.
9. Turtle's name.
12. Turtle's classification.
13. The name of the drink produced by Mr. Yarby's company.
16. Where they finally found Dribble.

WORD LIST: FOURTH GRADE NOTHING

ADVERTISING	FLOWERS	STAMPS
COMMERCIAL	FUDGE	TEETH
DICTIONARY	HOSPITAL	TRANSPORTATION
DOG	JUICY-O	TRAIN
DRIBBLE	MOVIES	TURTLE
FANG	PARTY	TUMMY
FISHBOWL	REPTILE	

ANSWERS: FOURTH GRADE NOTHING

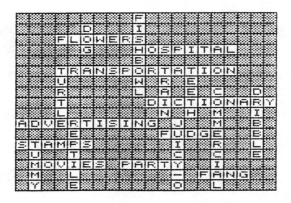

The Incredible Journey

by
Sheila Burnford

The Incredible Journey

by
Sheila Burnford

This story begins in the wilderness of northwestern Ontario. It involves three animals: an old bull terrier, a Siamese cat, and a young Labrador retriever.

The animals are staying with a friend of their owners while the latter are in England. When this friend leaves them to go on vacation, the three decide to travel several hundred miles back to their home.

As they are domestic animals, hunting for survival is a new experience for them. They encounter many hardships and dangerous situations during their travels. They also meet many well-meaning strangers who wish to befriend them, but nothing can deter them from their quest.

Chapters 1 and 2

VOCABULARY:

breadth	consoled
pulp	ferocity
amphibious	sybaritic barbarian
migratory	fretting
contrition	reciprocal
languished	gait
lope	eerie

KNOWLEDGE:

1. Where does the story take place?
2. Which one of the animals was a natural clown?
3. Explain why it was useless to shut the doors in the house.
4. The cat could only be defeated by what type of door handle?
5. How many members were there in the Hunter family?
6. Which person was considered the self-appointed owner of the cat?
7. Explain which animal was Peter's particular favorite. State your reason.
8. What are the names of the three animals?
9. Identify the sound for which the young dog always listened.

COMPREHENSION:

1. Describe the topography and population distribution of the area.
2. Which information shows you Mrs. Oakes's attitude and feelings regarding the animals? Mr. Longridge's?
3. Of the three, which animal knows how to manipulate humans most effectively?
4. Explain the term *godfather*.
5. Interpret why Longridge readily sympathized with the children over the separation from their pets.
6. Explain the quirk of fate that caused Mrs. Oakes to have the wrong opinion about where the animals have gone.
7. Relate the first responsive gesture Luath had ever given to Longridge.
8. Which animal appears to have taken on the role of protector?

APPLICATION:

1. Look up on a map of Canada the locale of this story. Obtain a class map and place a marker showing the animals' starting area. Continue placing markers along the route as their odyssey continues.
2. Research *Indian summer*. What does it mean? What are the weather conditions this time of year normally produces?
3. Choose one of the animals listed as being native to the area. Research information about it covering such items as natural habitat, migratory habits, and life cycles.
4. Change the written description of the phone conversation between Mr. Longridge and Mrs. Oakes to a dialogue for role playing. Keep in mind the condition of the telephone connection.

ANALYSIS:
1. Analyze whether or not you believe John Longridge was a rather reclusive man. Defend your opinion.
2. Referring to the description of the seasons given by the author, analyze and conclude how long the Indian summer will last as well as what the next season will entail.
3. Considering the three animals, which one would you consider to be the best pet for you? Explain.
4. Explain why you believe Siamese cats are often easier to train to a lead, whereas with other varieties it is contrary to their nature.

SYNTHESIS:
1. Choose one of the phrases describing the physical surroundings and sketch a picture illustrating it.
2. Write a description of each one of the three animals. Consider their physical appearance, age, strengths, and weaknesses.
3. Have Longridge write a letter to a friend explaining his unusual house guests and how their presence has altered his lifestyle.

EVALUATION:
1. All animals, just like humans, have their own way of coping with new situations. Evaluate the adjustment of each to their new lifestyle.
2. Appraise the strengths of each animal and how these qualities will assist them during the journey.

Chapters 3 and 4

VOCABULARY:

ravenous	whiskey-jack
gullet	facile
retched	indignity
enviously	talons
abhorrent	banshee
derelict	galvanizing
bleats	grotesque
whined	harlequin
succulent	immersion
forage	Ojibway
paroxysms	benevolent

KNOWLEDGE:
1. What did the terrier choose to eat that was familiar but didn't ease his hunger?
2. Explain why they didn't stay in the buildings they passed?
3. Why did the terrier lapse into unconsciousness?
4. Recount what caused the bear to leave Bodger alone.
5. What was Luath's first successful catch?
6. How did Tao make Bodger become interested in life again?

COMPREHENSION:
1. What prize do you think the cat had managed to catch?
2. How did the terrier eliminate the bad taste of the catch from his mouth?
3. Explain why the Labrador's heredity would make killing abhorrent to him.
4. What do you feel was causing the old dog to suffer from stiffness and an inability to move in the morning?
5. Tell how the Labrador tended the terrier's wounds.
6. Which one of the animals seems most uncomfortable around humans? Defend your opinion.

APPLICATION:
1. List some of the different varieties of trees described within these chapters.
2. Choosing at least two varieties from the aforementioned list, draw an example of each and label the various parts.
3. Tracking is vital for animal as well as human hunters. Research the tracks left by animals they might encounter during their trip. Copy and identify each set of prints in chart form.
4. Research and report on the Ojibway Indians. Include the legend of the "White Dog of Omen."

ANALYSIS:
1. Analyze the changing attitude of the Labrador towards the killing of other animals.
2. The cat's pattern was to growl whenever the terrier approached his kill. Interpret the change in his attitude and behavior when the dog was so ill.
3. Explain how the other animals changed their travel pattern to aid and protect Bodger while he was sick.
4. Analyze why the Indian women felt it was necessary to welcome the dog to their fireside.

SYNTHESIS:
1. Using the description given on page 31 (of the 1977 Bantam edition), create a picture illustrating the animals' surroundings and the beautifully colored fall foliage.
2. Create a different solution to the plight of the bull terrier.
3. After researching the "White Dog of Omen," draw your interpretation of it.

EVALUATION:
1. Each of the animals appears to feel a certain level of responsibility toward each other. Do we feel the same? Explain your opinion.
2. Judge the appropriateness and quality of illustrations in this book. Debate your answers.
3. Evaluate the value and need for maintaining wilderness areas. Have a class discussion.

Chapters 5 and 6

VOCABULARY:

endurance	hibernation	ravenously
unalterable	spasm	methodically
famished	incongruous	debris
ill-afforded	simian	impetus
forage	marauding	requiem
nomadic	bracken	subjection
lodestone	deference	pickerel
debonair	irresolute	austerity
expedition	fastidious	enigma
pigeonberry		

KNOWLEDGE:

1. Which animal was proving to be the best hunter?
2. Explain why the young dog wasn't a natural hunter.
3. Considering all three were animals with fur coats, explain which one will feel the cold the most. Give the reason for your opinion.
4. How could they always tell when bears had recently been in the area?
5. Recall how many miles they could cover on a good day.
6. Which one of the three actually went out of his way to encounter humans?
7. Explain how the Labrador protected his freshly caught rabbit.
8. How did the terrier deal with the disappearance of the cat?

COMPREHENSION:

1. Explain why hollows under uprooted trees became their favorite sleeping areas.
2. Nature had given one of the three better protection as he was already naturally adapted to the extremes in the weather. Decide which one fit this description and give reasons for your decision.
3. Explain the circumstances leading up to the separation of Tao from the others.
4. Helvi's parents fully accepted Tao after he performed an especially thoughtful act. Explain.

APPLICATION:

1. Report the general disposition and changing health of the terrier.
2. These chapters have many new and interesting words. Have the class look up their definitions and then play a round-robin type of game. One version is to have two students compete by standing while the teacher gives the definition, and the first one to say the correct term moves over to the next player while the other person sits down. The person who is able to move the farthest wins. This technique may also be adapted to questions from the story.
3. List some of the signs which signaled the coming of winter.
4. Explain why the Labrador could hardly acknowledge the terrier's greeting.

ANALYSIS:

1. Considering the three animals, which breed possesses a more nomadic nature?
2. Do a character analysis of the old man who took them into his home for a meal. Cite examples that illustrated his mental stability.
3. Summarize the reasons for the writing of this story.
4. Compare the basic personalities and attitudes of the trio.

SYNTHESIS:

1. You and two friends are going to colonize a new area previously unknown to anyone. You will be traveling by foot over potentially treacherous territory. Due to weight and lack of space you are each allowed to take only ten items and may lead one animal if you so choose. Have the students form groups and decide what items and animals they would take. Compare answers and discuss their reasons for the decisions.
2. Create a journal as if you were one of the three major characters. Describe one of the adventures they've had so far from that animal's viewpoint.
3. Develop a word search using the vocabulary list. The definitions could be the clues.
4. Write a descriptive poem about either one of the animals or all three.

EVALUATION:

1. Discuss how well a human could survive in that wilderness. What would be some real areas of concern?
2. Evaluate how you think animals learn. Do they think? Debate your answers.
3. The animals were shot at while trying to forage for food in a garbage pail. Judge whether or not you feel the man was within his rights. Does your knowledge of the animals' situation influence your judgment in this matter?
4. Judge why Helvi's parents never kept any animal that didn't "earn its keep."

Chapters 7 and 8

VOCABULARY:

apparition	culprit
avowed	dervish
capitulated	molybdenum
sallied	pliant
bittern	detested
elongated	wanton
voraciously	somersaulted
ecstatic	

KNOWLEDGE:

1. Tell why the terrier wasn't a successful hunter.
2. What is a good fight considered to be for a terrier?
3. The bull terrier's eyes were said to resemble those of another creature when he was involved in a fight. What was that creature?
4. What job was traditionally given to Siamese cats in old Siam?

5. The Siamese cat and the old dog had been united in their common dislike of a certain species of animal. What was that species?

COMPREHENSION:
1. Explain how the food they have been eating has affected the Labrador's physical condition.
2. Tell what helped restore the old dog's morale.
3. Describe the quills of a porcupine and how they "throw" them.
4. Relate the story which explains the reason for the crook at the end of a Siamese cat's tail.
5. Explain the special bonding that had occurred between the cat and the terrier.
6. Recount the incident with the duck blind. What did this show about the cat's attitude?

APPLICATION:
1. Construct a diorama of either an incident or merely showing the animals during their journey.
2. Look up the term *molybdenum*. Give a report to the class about the metal and its uses.
3. List some of the ways the young dog attempted to dislodge the quills. Was he successful?
4. Using the given information about Siamese cats as a basis, collect unusual facts about these animals. Share your information with the class.
5. Research information about Siam. Report on various interesting facts including what the country is currently called and why the name was changed.

ANALYSIS:
1. Compare and contrast one of the animals and his personality to either your own pet or one you know.
2. The Siamese cat was one of the family unitl his hearing returned. Explain why, in your opinion, the return of this sense created a difference in him.
3. Analyze why the cat was careful to cover all traces of his passing through the area. How much resulted from concern for his current situation and how much involved pure instinct?

SYNTHESIS:
1. Create a Missing Animals poster showing the three animals. Be certain to include their pictures, characteristics, and any other information that might help to identify them.
2. Draw a picture of Tao while he was living with Helvi.
3. These animals readily learned to adapt to their new surroundings. Design and construct a maze for a hamster, mouse, or similar pet animal. Conduct training experiments. Keep a record of your results.

EVALUATION:
1. In chapters 3 and 4 the cat's concern for the old dog was obvious. This section explained more of the reasons behind the friendship between the two animals. Judge how commonality of experience and facing adversity would affect this type of relationship.
2. The beginning of the story leads toward the belief that the Labrador would be the protector. Subsequently the others have been even more successful in coming to the aid of their comrades. Evaluate how this scenario equates to interpersonal relationships.

Chapters 9 through 11

VOCABULARY:

unscathed	catastrophe	disreputable
tote	ominous	simultaneously
hamlets	precarious	pathetic
primeval	wheaton	rime
porcine	ramble	gallivanting
gargoyle	sublimely	unquenchable
infinitesimal	implicit	diligent
piteous	mutinous	surreptitiously
laggard	cornucopia	

KNOWLEDGE:

1. Which one of the three animals was in the worst condition by this point in the story?
2. What was the registered name of the terrier?
3. How did the dogs manage to get out of the locked stable?
4. In which compass direction had the animals traveled?
5. What did Elizabeth bring as a souvenir for Tao?
6. Explain Pete's attitude toward his giving Bodger a present.
7. Which member of the family was the first to hear the returning animals?
8. What signal did Mr. Hunter give to discover if Luath was in the vicinity?

COMPREHENSION:

1. Explain the reason behind the deterioration of Luath.
2. Why did the senior forester feel his associate might have been imagining things when he mentioned seeing the trio?
3. Relate why a week later the junior forester's sighting was justified.
4. Describe Tao's reaction to Elizabeth.
5. Explain why at first Peter was so dejected.

APPLICATION:

1. Research the Strellon Game Reserve. Report on its location and terrain.
2. Continue marking on the map the different locations the animals have traveled. Skim over the book to locate at the aforementioned areas, game reserves, towns, etc.
3. Be a detective. From the information Mr. Longridge has uncovered recording sightings of the trio, follow their route home. How close is this to the routing you developed in the previous question?

ANALYSIS:

1. There is a video of *The Incredible Journey*. After viewing it, critique it both on its own worth and in comparison to the book. Using particular incidents, compare the author's description to the interpretation given to it in the film.
2. Analyze why the names of the animals were used in the first chapters by the author and then never repeated until the conclusion.
3. Compare the attitudes and feelings of the three members of the Hunter family who felt one of the lost pets was primarily theirs.

SYNTHESIS:
1. This book does not have a title for each chapter. Create one for each based on the material in that chapter.
2. Create a comic strip to retell the story.
3. Compose a letter from Mr. Longridge to Mr. Hunter explaining the disappearance of the animals.
4. Role play the scene between Mrs. Oakes and Mr. Longridge where they are piecing together the animals departure as well as voicing their concerns for their safety.

EVALUATION:
1. Read the book *Old Yeller* by Fred Gipson (New York: Harper and Row, 1956) and compare it to this story. Evaluate the similarities and lessons learned.
2. The animals were extremely faithful to each other. Do you feel this is an important trait for everyone or not. Explain your opinion.
3. Have a class discussion regarding the hunting of animals. Divide the class into debating teams with opposing points of view.
4. Analyze the last sentence of the book: "It was Tao, returning for his old friend, that they might end their journey together." Discuss your interpretation of that sentence and how well it sums up the entire story.

Additional Activities

ART:
1. Make a booklet with drawings of different flora and fauna native to the northwestern part of Canada.
2. Create a collage composed of pictures of the different animals the trio encountered during their journey.
3. Design a mobile which hangs from a center drawing of one of the principal animals. Suspend from it other drawings that either illustrate key qualities or incidents which occurred to it. (Laminating the pictures will allow them to hang easier.)
4. Create masks using a basic form and papier-mâché to form the heads of the animals. Be creative in the use of paint, artificial fur, etc., to develop the best effect for each.

DRAMA:
1. Broadway recently had a very successful show which dealt exclusively with one type of animal. Create a play about this book with students performing the animal characterizations. Be certain to study animals for mannerisms and natural habits which would add credence to each performance.
2. Using the masks created in art activity 4, role play the animals discussing their journey after they are safely at home.
3. Perform an oral reading of a scene you found particularly interesting or expressive.
4. Prepare an all-points police bulletin regarding the missing threesome.

WRITING:
1. Have the students write a new adventure for the animals. Alter the circumstances by either including a new animal or replacing one of the existing ones.
2. Write a sequel to the story.
3. An interesting but surprisingly difficult concept is to reduce something to a minimum but still retain its meaning. Using one sentence per chapter, recount the story.
4. Write a newspaper article of the travels of these animals and their safe return home. Give it an interesting headline designed to get people to read the article.
5. Have the students create an acrostic using one of the animals either by breed or name.

MUSIC:
1. A ballad is a form of narrative poetry told through song. They have been used throughout history to tell events both real and imaginary. Using facts from this story, create one about the animals and their journey and set it to either a childhood or currently popular melody.
2. Have the students form small groups to choose a book passage that expresses either strong emotion or is descriptive in nature. Choose a musical selection which expresses the emotions and feelings of the passage. Record the music and use it as a background while reading the section to the rest of the class.

SCIENCE/SOCIAL STUDIES:
1. You have followed the trek of the animals through the Canadian wilderness. Utilizing the map scale, compute land miles traveled and see how closely it compares to the stated numbers given in the book.
2. Using the same map compare the direct distance between the two points to the previous computation.
3. Research the history of the three breeds of animals. Present a short report to the class.
4. Make a leaf collection with examples of as many different leaves as possible. Using a botany guide for that area of Canada, label them, press them, and place them in a scrapbook.

Bulletin Board

1. Each student is to choose at least one animal either domestic or wild and write a short story or poem about it.

2. The focus should be either biographical in nature or an adventure it supposedly experienced.

3. They are to draw a picture to illustrate their creative writing.

The Pinballs

by
Betsy Byars

The Pinballs

by

Betsy Byars

The Pinballs, by Betsy Byars, focuses on the problems and ultimate triumph of three foster children. They are Carlie, Harvey, and Thomas J.

Each child has been disappointed and neglected by his or her parents. Carlie terms them *pinballs* because pinballs cannot help themselves. Her bitterness is evidenced through sarcasm and cynicism. Harvey's father has "accidentally" driven over his son's legs leaving him deeply despondent. Thomas J. has lived with elderly twins, removed from companions except for the eccentric spinsters.

Mr. and Mrs. Mason, as foster parents, help each of the children to grow in special ways. At Mrs. Mason's request, Carlie determines to bring Harvey out of his depression. Her method, although unorthodox, does help him gain a better perspective. In order to help Thomas J., Mr. Mason relates his own fears and struggles of childhood. Along with Carlie and Harvey, the boy begins to grow and find his own identity.

Real progress has occurred when Carlie announces that she and the other children are no longer pinballs. Pinballs can't help what happens to them and don't try—the opposite of the foster children after they spend a few months with the Masons. Realistic and poignant, the story illustrates vividly the importance of nurturing and self-esteem in a caring environment.

Chapters 1 and 2

VOCABULARY:

congratulations   concussion
authorities   social worker
stabilize

KNOWLEDGE:
1. Tell why the happiest day in Harvey's life turned into the saddest day.
2. Who had rescued Thomas J.?
3. How are Carlie's responses different from the other children?
4. Why did the Benson twins not notify the authorities about Thomas J.? List two reasons.
5. Tell the reasons that the court had taken Carlie, Thomas J., and Harvey away from their parents.

COMPREHENSION:
1. Describe Harvey's feelings when his father decided to go to the poker game instead of the essay award meeting.
2. Explain why Harvey's essay title, "Why I am Proud to be an American," was ironic.
3. Why did Carlie feel that "stabilizing" her home was a social worker's hopeless dream?
4. Describe the events that followed after Russell hit Carlie.
5. Tell why Carlie doesn't believe Harvey's explanation of his broken legs.
6. Identify two reasons why Carlie was suspicious of people.

APPLICATION:
1. What would you have done about your parents if you had been Carlie, Harvey, or Thomas J.? Write a telegram in a secret code to a partner explaining your plan.
2. Relate the story from the point of view of Russell, Harvey's father, and the Benson twins.
3. Because you know that each of the children has definite skills, list two ways that each could make living at the Mason's a more comfortable and/or exciting experience.
4. How can you use your special skills, like imagination, to help either yourself or someone else who is having a problem? Can you think of an unusual solution for the problem?
5. Pretend that you are Carlie, Thomas J., or Harvey. How would a game that you have played or a book that you have read have altered the way that you feel about your life? Make a reading list for each of the children that might help them.

ANALYSIS:
1. Write to a newspaper advice column. As the children, you need immediate answers to your problems. Your partner can reply with various solutions.
2. Compare Carlie's favorite television shows to life with her stepfather. How are they alike? Different?
3. With a classmate, discuss the possibility of Harvey telling Carlie the truth about his broken legs. How would this have changed the story?
4. Find a newspaper article that tells how a foster parent, social worker, or other individual in the helping professions has contributed to the community.

SYNTHESIS:
1. Draw a cartoon of Carlie as she would have looked in the row of foster children photographs. Use dialogue to describe her first impressions of the Mason home.
2. Organize a skit which resembles the scene between Carlie and Harvey.
3. Draw individual pictures of Mrs. Mason as each of the children would have wanted her to look. Remember each one's past experiences.
4. Create titles for chapters 1 and 2 that best summarizes the action and feelings.
5. Editorials can persuade or inform. Write an editorial about the children and their parent problems for class discussion.
6. Design a bumper sticker using words and symbols for each of the children.
7. Create a congratulations card for each of the three children and Mrs. Mason. Focus on a unique personality trait of each.

EVALUATION:
1. Decide which of the children has the deepest problems and why. Make a chart expressing your opinions.
2. Compare each child's background by writing a cinquain poem. Judge which was the most caring.
3. Decide on an object that you could take to a foster home that would best reflect your personality.

Chapters 3 and 4

VOCABULARY:
technique
vaccine
basin

KNOWLEDGE:
1. Why did Thomas J. talk so loud?
2. Where did Thomas J. discover the earring?
3. Recall the reason that Harvey could not insult Carlie.
4. Why did Thomas J. like to find objects for Carlie and the Benson twins?
5. Describe Carlie's "sickness," which occurred during her first night at the Masons.

COMPREHENSION:
1. Explain how Carlie's truthful admission to Mrs. Mason concerning her homesickness changed their relationship.
2. How did the Benson twins' injuries occur?
3. Explain how Thomas J.'s name was part of a family tradition.
4. Describe the incident that aroused the Bensons' anger toward Thomas J.

APPLICATION:
1. Write a diary entry. Tell about a time in your life when you had to adjust to a new situation. Describe your initial feelings and reactions.

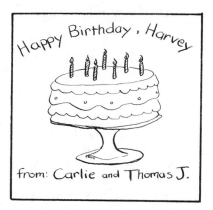

ANALYSIS:

1. Compare and contrast Carlie's reaction to Thomas J. finding the earring to what he expected. Recall past experiences that led to the confrontation.
2. Analyze Thomas J.'s feelings. How did the way he felt about his hair as compared to Carlie's sum up his overall feelings about himself?
3. Compare the children in this story to those in *Where the Lilies Bloom* by Vera Cleaver. How were they alike? Different?
4. Thomas J. was compared to a blind pig. Think of other images that would describe him.

SYNTHESIS:

1. Design a Wanted — A Home poster for each of the children. Illustrate the ideal home and family that each dreams of.
2. Create a paper cast such as Harvey would have worn. Each student signs it and writes a message that will have a special meaning for Harvey.
3. How else could Mrs. Mason, Thomas J., and Harvey have reacted to Carlie's disrespectful attitude? Write a different ending for the chapter using your ideas.

EVALUATION:

1. Judge your feelings about the children's parents. Create a short script of a courtroom scene in which each parent appears. As judge, determine an individual rehabilitation plan that will also benefit the children.
2. Research qualities of leadership and make notes of your findings. Evaluate why Carlie is emerging as the children's natural leader.

Chapters 5 through 8

VOCABULARY:
    commune
    identify
    appendectomy
    yoga

KNOWLEDGE:
1. Who did Carlie want to call instead of her mother?
2. Why did Carlie refer to the children as pinballs?
3. State the reason that Harvey's father had cried at the hospital.
4. What was the title of the first list that Harvey wrote?

COMPREHENSION:
1. Explain why Carlie felt uncomfortable if anyone was polite or friendly with her.
2. How did Carlie's reading choices reflect her career goals?
3. Was Carlie really sick of "The Young and Restless"? Explain.
4. Describe Harvey's feelings as he attempted to compose his first letter.

APPLICATION:
1. Have you ever formed a mistaken impression about someone that had to be revised after learning more about the person? Share your experience with a partner.
2. What parts of chapter 5 or 6 would you have found embarrassing, frightening, or funny? Explain by writing about similar experiences.
3. Harvey's lists of "Books That I Have Enjoyed and Bad Things That Have Happened to Me" had a special purpose—they helped the children find common interests. Compose a list of your choices to share with a classmate.

ANALYSIS:
1. Compare and contrast Harvey and Carlie's feelings about missing the essay contest and the Miss Teenage Lancaster contest. How are they alike? Different?
2. Explain why Carlie's fantasies aid in creating inner strength while Harvey's result in weakness.

SYNTHESIS:
1. Create a composite illustration of Carlie and Harvey showing fantasies of themselves. Perhaps a nurse's uniform and a football uniform could be included. Create another illustration portraying them as they actually appeared at the foster home.
2. Make a commercial advertising the services of Carlie as a nurse, Harvey as a star quarterback, or Thomas J. as a famous sleuth.
3. Carlie would have liked to have been an Appalachian nurse. If you could assume the identity of a person from a favorite book, movie, or play, who would it be? Write a short story with you as the main character. Focus on your character's occupation.
4. Practice ad-lib. Imagine a meeting between a nurse, football player, and a detective. Create a scene where something humorous, then frightening occurs. Use your ad-lib scene to launch individual or class short stories.

EVALUATION:

1. List five qualities that foster parents should have. Decide whether Mrs. Mason possesses these qualities.
2. Judge which child's personality reminds you of yourself or someone you know. Explain in one paragraph.

Chapters 9 through 12

VOCABULARY:

guinea pig
principle
abandoned

KNOWLEDGE:

1. Recall the reason that Harvey is "addicted" to Kentucky Fried Chicken.
2. Give the reason that Mrs. Mason became a social worker.
3. What were the valuable articles that Thomas J. was to take from the Benson home?
4. Name the gifts that Carlie and Harvey wanted most.

COMPREHENSION:

1. Explain why Carlie told Harvey that he had hope after he ordered her to go into the house.
2. Retell the events in chapter 12 in your own words.
3. Why was Carlie curious about what bugged people?
4. Explain why Thomas J. felt strange holding the twins' hands.

APPLICATION:

1. Role play a conversation that the Benson twins might have had concerning Thomas J.'s future after he left the hospital.
2. Harvey's father resented his having a gerbil because it reminded him of Harvey's mother. Relate instances when past experiences have colored your reactions. Share your experiences with a partner.
3. Interview the twins to find out about their amusing experiences exchanging roles. Learn if they have a special communication system.
4. Draw a picture of the twins in the hospital as they must have appeared to Thomas J.

ANALYSIS:

1. Think of the main problems that Carlie and Harvey must face. Identify barriers that they will confront before becoming a nurse or a quarterback. Chart the course that you perceive for each. Contrast this to your own goals.
2. What in Carlie's past encouraged her to learn from Mrs. Mason, as a teacher?
3. Compare and contrast Thomas J.'s life in an almost totally silent environment to that of his foster home. As Thomas J., describe the differences in a letter to the Benson twins.

SYNTHESIS:
1. Carlie chose to become a nurse although she had known little care. Compose a diamante contrasting her home life to the future that she imagines in a medical career.
2. Construct a paper banner for Carlie, Harvey, and Thomas J. Include words of encouragement and references to their daily triumphs.
3. What if Carlie had run away and Harvey had "rolled" away? Create a new adventure. Videotape your presentations.
4. Create a book cover based on the story so far. Illustrate unique aspects of each character's personality.

EVALUATION:
1. Harvey and Carlie initially formed negative opinions based on first impressions. Did their impressions concerning each other and Mrs. Mason last? Explain.
2. What was the most important quality in the Mason's care? How did this quality foster growth in the children? Explain.

Chapters 13 through 16

VOCABULARY:
hygiene
cosmopolitan
juvenile

KNOWLEDGE:
1. Explain why Harvey searched for a newspaper article about his mother.
2. Why does Carlie think that the wheelchair will make running away easier?
3. State the reasons that Jefferson Benson died.
4. Where does Harvey think that his mother will take him when she learns about his broken legs?

COMPREHENSION:
1. Tell why Harvey suddenly disclosed the secret concerning his broken legs to Carlie.
2. Discuss why Carlie is a caring person even though her words are sharp.
3. Tell the reason that Carlie tried to convince Harvey that his fifteen minutes would be spent as a famous writer.
4. Explain how Harvey must have felt when he saw the photograph of his mother at the farm.

APPLICATION:
1. When Carlie learned that Harvey's father was responsible for his broken legs she must have remembered her stepfather. Write about a time when you empathized with someone due to a similar experience.
2. Harvey thought that everyone has fifteen minutes to be famous. Tape record an account of your most famous minutes of the past and/or future.

ANALYSIS:
1. Compare and contrast Harvey's father when he initially met Harvey, to Harvey's father in the restaurant. Analyze the reasons for the abrupt change.
2. Identify an event in the story that represents a turning point in Harvey and his father's relationship.
3. Analyze the response of Harvey's father concerning his wife's letters. Was it insensitive or kind? Explain.
4. Recall the scene when Harvey's father arrived. Think of one word to describe each of the following: Carlie, Harvey, and Harvey's father.

SYNTHESIS:
1. Create a newspaper headline and story. Write about your own special encounter like that of Harvey, Thomas J., and Carlie. Tell what changes this relationship has brought to your life.
2. In cartoon format, block the action for chapters 15 and 16.
3. Develop a different plan by which Harvey can contact his mother.

EVALUATION:
1. What did Harvey say that expressed his deepest despair?
2. Predict what would have happened if Harvey's father had helped him write a letter to his mother.
3. Why did Carlie suddenly surprise Mrs. Mason with a request for work? Determine other positive outlets for her anger.

Chapters 17 through 19

VOCABULARY:
coffin
feeble
respect
decals

KNOWLEDGE:
1. What worried Thomas J. about going to the hospital?
2. Why did Harvey stop laughing at Carlie's jokes?
3. Identify the emotion felt by Aunt Benson when she realized that there would not be a double funeral.
4. Why did Thomas J. suddenly feel that he had stepped into real life?

COMPREHENSION:
1. Describe what Carlie had done to help Harvey although he seemed momentarily worse.
2. Why did Mr. Mason share his frightening funeral experience with Thomas J.?
3. Give two reasons for the change in Harvey's behavior.
4. Retell chapter 19 in three sentences—one for the beginning, middle, and end.

APPLICATION:
1. Like Harvey, have you ever felt trapped by a problem until discussing the matter with someone you trusted? Share your experiences with a partner.
2. Aunt Benson was lonely without her twin sister. Recall someone that you miss. Write a haiku and illustrate one of your happiest memories.
3. Harvey was disappointed when he received a television set instead of a puppy for his birthday. Design a birthday card that you would have appreciated had you been Harvey.

ANALYSIS:
1. How was Mr. Mason's relationship with his mother much like that of Thomas J.'s with the twins? Give two examples.
2. Ramona Mason was different from her husband in her ability to express love. Explain how she came to be a model for Mr. Mason and Thomas J.
3. Summarize the main theme of *The Pinballs* in one sentence.
4. What advice as a friend would you give to Harvey to help him to become more outgoing and less self absorbed?

SYNTHESIS:
1. If you had been Carlie would you have been intimidated by Harvey's father? Role play a telephone conversation telling what you know about his son and how he can help.
2. Harvey is seeking love so desperately he doesn't realize that he is surrounded by it. As Harvey, write a postcard to the other characters telling them that you are willing to try to give more instead of always taking in future relationships.
3. Create mobiles with symbols of the caring and friendship expressed in *The Pinballs*.

EVALUATION:
1. If you had been Harvey would you have allowed someone else to open your birthday present? Did this passive attitude have a deeper meaning? Discuss with a classmate.
2. Do you think Carlie was sincere when she volunteered to go to the Virginia farm? Why or why not?
3. Judge what would have happened to Harvey if Carlie had not discovered his swollen toes.

Chapters 20 through 23

VOCABULARY:
opal
viruses
hula
contract

KNOWLEDGE:
1. Explain why Thomas J. doesn't know the date of his birthday.
2. Tell the reason that Harvey cried when he saw the puppy.
3. Relate Carlie's number one rule when she becomes a nurse.

4. Recall the emotion that Thomas J. felt when he was sworn to secrecy concerning the puppy.

COMPREHENSION:
1. Why was Harvey so intense about permanently keeping the puppy?
2. Describe the change in Harvey when he realized that the puppy was really his.
3. Tell why the children wanted a puppy that was a "licker."
4. Explain why the nurse chose to ignore Harvey's birthday present.

APPLICATION:
1. Carlie and Thomas J. felt like failures as *cheerer uppers*. With a classmate think of an unusual method to cheer up Harvey or someone that you know in the hospital.
2. Tell about the events in chapter 23 from the nurse's point of view.
3. Find written accounts of pets that have performed heroic deeds. Share the information with your class.

ANALYSIS:
1. Explain why Carlie was courageous in taking responsibility for her decisions.
2. How would you describe the relationship between Carlie and Thomas J. at the end of chapter 23?
3. How did the children select the best puppy? List the qualities that you would want in a pet.
4. Carlie could be described as generous in chapter 20. What one word would best describe her in chapter 21?

SYNTHESIS:
1. Design an ideal hospital room. Include everything that you would want in your own private room.
2. Create a make-believe animal. Use your animal in a fantasy or futuristic story.
3. Imagine that the children had found Harvey happy and improved in the hospital. What might have happened? Explain in one paragraph.
4. Practice brainstorming. Discuss a current classroom problem. Think of many solutions. Decide on a practical but unique plan of action.

EVALUATION:
1. Determine what was the most important lesson that the children learned from the hospital experience.
2. Judge which scenes from the book would best show the children's inner growth. Create a mural to illustrate your ideas.
3. Harvey's father is the only parent that visited one of the children. Judge whether his motivation was positive or negative. Defend your opinions in a group discussion.
4. *The Pinballs* is realistic fiction. List the elements that are found in realistic fiction.

Chapters 24 through 26

VOCABULARY:
cameo
professional
decorette
resembled

KNOWLEDGE:
1. Recall how Carlie planned to tell Mrs. Mason about the puppy.
2. What was Thomas J.'s first compliment?
3. What kind of school would Carlie like to attend?
4. Describe Thomas J.'s ideal mother.

COMPREHENSION:
1. Explain why Carlie feels "famous."
2. Why did Thomas J. find it so difficult to express love?
3. Identify two reasons why Carlie thought that Mrs. Mason would accept the puppy.
4. Explain why Thomas J. felt his first real sadness about Thomas Benson's death while in the barbershop.

APPLICATION:
1. Carlie believed that when you really try you are not a pinball. Write about an experience in your life based upon this belief.
2. Use information from chapter 26 to construct a diorama. Include the schools as symbols of hope to the children.
3. Each child is learning to trust again. Demonstrate an individual or group game in which trust is the focus.
4. Discuss why first impressions cannot always be trusted. Cite examples from *The Pinballs*.
5. Decide how you would treat the children if they came to your school. Make notes of ways that you would welcome them. Use some of the plans to welcome newcomers to your classroom.

ANALYSIS:
1. View the video production of *The Pinballs*. Would you make any changes to more closely follow the plot of the book? Write notes of your opinions for a class discussion.
2. Why was a pinball a particularly descriptive word for the children?
3. In what areas did Mr. and Mrs. Mason and the children show the most improvement? Create a Most Improved award for each.
4. Suppose that Harvey and Carlie return to their homes to find parents that have not changed. How would their year at the Masons help them to cope? Explain.

SYNTHESIS:

1. Predict what will happen during the next school year. Pretend that you are one of the children. Write a journal entry about your new experiences.
2. Name something unusual that Harvey would have liked for a birthday present. Explain your choice.
3. Design a Getting Acquainted poster for one of the foster children. Include illustrations of his or her interests, career choices, books, etc.
4. Role play a Parents Day at the new school. Interview Mrs. Mason to find out about some of her most exciting moments with the children.

EVALUATION:

1. Judge which of the foster children formed the deepest friendships. Explain your opinion in a class discussion.
2. Give an oral reading of a portion of the book that you consider your favorite or a turning point in the story.

Additional Activities

ART:

1. Using stencil paper cut a stencil of an object representing Carlie, Harvey, or Thomas J. An example is Harvey's puppy. Place the stencil over a sheet of paper. Dip a small sponge into tempura paint and press lightly over the stencil.
2. Create a paper mosaic depicting a favorite scene in the story. Make a pencil drawing of the scene on paper. Cut colored paper into uniform squares. Leaving a margin between each square, glue each to the drawing.

DRAMA:

1. Act out a favorite scene from the story and videotape it. Choose a scene with intense interaction between characters.
2. Act out the same scene but with the time changed either to the year 2050 or to early colonial days.
3. Compare the two videotapes to see how time influences action.

CREATIVE WRITING:

1. Write a letter to Betsy Byars expressing your opinion of *The Pinballs*.
2. Write a mystery story with the setting at the new school. Include Harvey, Carlie, and the new puppy.

MUSIC:

1. Find recorded music that would represent each character. For example, Carlie's theme might be a rock and roll song. Play the music softly while reading aloud a section which best represents the character.

SCIENCE:

1. Find information about dogs used for special purposes such as seeing eye or police dogs. Make notes to report your findings to the class.

SOCIAL STUDIES:

1. Learn more about foster home care. Interview a foster parent and/or a social worker. Ask questions that the class has composed.
2. Research famous people that have reached their goals in spite of personal obstacles. Find the common reasons that they became successful.
3. If the characters in *The Pinballs* had shared their diaries or journals the Masons could have learned much about their past lives. Research to find out if a famous person you admire has kept a diary or journal. Share the most interesting excerpts with the class.
4. Find information about Clara Barton and Florence Nightingale. Learn about their childhoods and how it may have affected their choice of careers.
5. Learn about genealogy and trace your family background. Find out if your family came from a foreign country. Perhaps an ancestor was named after a famous historical person like the Benson twins.
6. The problem of homeless adults and children has become an ever increasing challenge for metropolitan areas. Research current news magazines and newspapers to find methods used to aid the homeless. Report to your class.

Bulletin Board

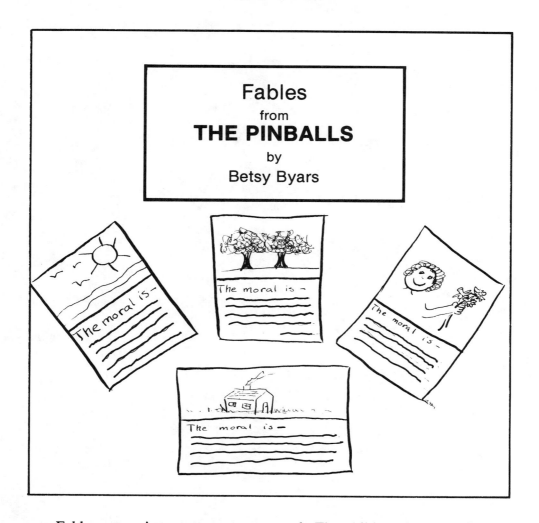

Fables are written to express a moral. The children in *The Pinballs* learned many lessons. Each student writes a fable based on a lesson learned in the book, a new pinball adventure, or a personal experience. Illustrate and state the moral as shown.

Shoeshine Girl

by
Clyde Robert Bulla

Shoeshine Girl

by
Clyde Robert Bulla

Unruly ten-year-old Sarah Ida has been sent to Aunt Claudia's home for the summer. She angrily rejects all attempts at friendship. Aunt Claudia introduces her to Rossi, a generous and trusting child. Later she discovers that Sarah Ida has "borrowed" all of Rossi's money. The resulting confrontation leaves Sarah Ida more determined to assert her independence and find a job.

Al, the shoeshine man, would have been the girl's next victim had he not been so patient and wise. After he hires Sarah Ida as the shoeshine girl, he teaches her many lessons about the value of relationships and money. Through his gentle, but straight-forward guidance, she learns that friendship and inner action are more important than the possession of money.

A final episode relates the child's emotional growth during the summer. Sarah Ida's parents ask that she come home to additional responsibility due to a family crisis. She weighs the decision to return home very carefully. Finally, she decides that she is prepared for the challenge due to her experiences with Al and Rossi. Tough, self-reliant, but more sensitive and caring, the shoeshine girl is doing as Al advised — becoming more prepared.

Chapters 1 and 2

VOCABULARY:
>   fussy
>   creepy

KNOWLEDGE:
1.   What kind of room did Sarah Ida prefer?
2.   Recall why Sarah Ida is spending the summer with her aunt.
3.   Who was Midge?
4.   Why did Sarah Ida start to unpack?
5.   What did Rossi have that Sarah Ida "borrowed"?

COMPREHENSION:
1.   Describe Sarah Ida's feelings when Aunt Claudia asked if she always gave her parents reason to trust her.
2.   Why was Aunt Claudia not supposed to pay Sarah Ida for anything?
3.   Explain the reason that Sarah Ida was determined to have money in her pocket.
4.   Why did Aunt Claudia give Sarah Ida a sharp look?
5.   What do you think Sarah Ida was thinking when she told Rossi not to mention the money?

APPLICATION:
1.   Tell a partner about a time when you wanted money but had none. Describe your solution to the problem.
2.   Pretend that you are Rossi when Sarah threatened to leave. What would your reply have been?
3.   If the bank had contained one hundred dollars, how would the story have changed? Write a new ending for chapter 2 describing the events.
4.   Read *The Midas Touch*. Pretend as Aunt Claudia that you try to teach Sarah Ida the moral of the story.
5.   Sarah Ida was probably influenced by advertisement. Survey your class to see what is the favorite or most effective advertisement for children. Chart the results.

ANALYSIS:
1.   Think of five paying jobs that Sarah Ida could create for herself. As a class, share ideas of ways that children can make money with unusual jobs. Record your responses.
2.   Why did Sarah Ida not feel guilty about taking Rossi's money?
3.   How was borrowing money like a game to Midge?
4.   Analyze the events in Sarah Ida's and Rossi's pasts. Why was Sarah Ida self-interested while Rossi was more interested in others?
5.   Read *Summer of the Monkeys* by Wilson Rawls. How were Aunt Claudia and Grandpa's philosophies concerning money alike?

SYNTHESIS:

1. If you were to live away from home for a summer, what would you take that would be a conversation piece? Design a toy or a game that best represents your personality.
2. Create a Miss Manners guide for Sarah Ida. Illustrate courteous responses to adults and friends.
3. Role play a scene in which Sarah Ida and Midge are discovered stealing a dress. As the store detective, you will interview them and, later, consult their parents.
4. Read *The Giving Tree* by Shel Silverstein. Tape record Rossi, Midge, and Sarah Ida's opinions of the story.
5. One of the themes of *Shoeshine Girl* is that happiness can better be found with friends than with money. Write a modern fairy tale expressing the theme. Use the main characters or ones that you create.
6. The cab driver and Rossi appear to accept Sarah Ida's sullen and devious behavior. What are they really thinking? Create a paragraph of *self-talk* for each. Compare your ideas with those of your class.

EVALUATION:

1. Do you think that Sarah Ida will learn a lesson about friendship in this story? Determine a way to teach a lesson about friendship through gentleness instead of force. Share your ideas.
2. View the video production of *Shoeshine Girl*. Which character is closest to your imagined version? Explain.
3. Design a new wardrobe for Sarah Ida. Role play her first meeting with Rossi wearing patched clothes. In a second role play, judge whether she has a more positive attitude in the new wardrobe.
4. Judge how long it would have taken Sarah Ida and Rossi to double their money if they had invested it. Find information about compound interest. Share the information by reporting to the class.
5. If you had been Sarah Ida's parents, how would you have taught her not to "borrow" or steal? Determine a method that would be fun but effective.
6. Judge why Sarah Ida was impatient to have money while Aunt Claudia was calm and practical about her having it.

Chapters 3 and 4

VOCABULARY:
advantage
relation

KNOWLEDGE:

1. Who discovered that Rossi's money was missing?
2. Where did Sarah Ida hide the money?
3. Why did the pet shop owner not hire the girl?
4. How did Sarah Ida decide to earn money?
5. What emotion did Aunt Claudia display when her lips tightened?
6. What part of Sarah Ida's name did Al recognize?

COMPREHENSION:
1. Describe the person Al hoped to hire to shine shoes.
2. Explain why Sarah Ida thought that Aunt Claudia would never allow her to take the job.
3. Describe the events in the story after Sarah Ida walked away from Al.
4. Why didn't Sarah Ida apply for a job in the dress shop?
5. Give two reasons why most people didn't want to work for Al.
6. How did Sarah Ida know that she could take advantage of Rossi?

APPLICATION:
1. Think about a time in your life when you were discouraged. Did someone give you a chance to prove yourself? Create a poem constructed so that the words depict a shape relevant to your experience. For example, if a kite was important in your experience, the words of the poem would be in the shape of a kite.
2. Children can also earn money. Create a poster advertising your services. Research advertisement techniques before you begin.
3. Read *The Toothpaste Millionaire* by Jean Merrill. Find out how to start a business of your own. Make notes to share with your class.
4. Invite a coin collector to your class. Find out about valuable coins and how to start a coin collection.

ANALYSIS:
1. Sarah Ida and Rossi were both embarrassed when the money was returned. Why did they react so differently? Explain.
2. Explain why Al trusted Sarah Ida more when he realized she was staying with Aunt Claudia.
3. Make a short job resumé for Sarah Ida and Rossi. Compare the resumés to determine who would be the better shoeshine girl.
4. Analyze the last conversation between Aunt Claudia and her niece. How could the confrontation have been different so that they both "won"?

SYNTHESIS:
1. Create a collage using words and pictures from newspapers and magazines. Show a composite impression of the main characters. For example, Rossi's collage might include a bank, a recipe, and the word friendship.
2. The shoeshine stand was a symbol of independence and achievement for Sarah Ida. Make a papier-mâché or clay figure of your symbol of achievement.
3. A famous saying is "A penny saved is a penny earned." Write and illustrate a simple picture book explaining the concept to younger students.
4. Pretend that you are Grandmother Sarah Ida. Tell your grandchildren how and why you became a shoeshine girl.
5. Al's profession was unique and old-fashioned. Interview a person that you admire in an unusual profession. Share the information that you learn with your class.
6. Create a full-size model of Al's shoeshine stand from corrugated cardboard. Use as a backdrop for role plays.
7. Sketch a picture of the next problem you think Sarah Ida will face with Aunt Claudia or Al. Compare with classmates' ideas.

EVALUATION:

1. Judge which fear disappeared after Sarah Ida talked to Al.
2. Compare Aunt Claudia's first impression of her niece to her later impression. Judge which is the more realistic. Why?
3. If you were Aunt Claudia, would you allow your niece to take the job? List the positive and negative reasons. Compare and determine your decision.
4. How could Aunt Claudia have stopped the girl from running away? What would you have done in the same situation?
5. Debate whether it is better to learn from experience or advice.
6. Predict how Sarah Ida will change after taking a job.
7. Determine how Sarah Ida is changing a frustrating situation into a more productive one.
8. Explain how having a job and earning money can change a person's attitude toward the value of money.
9. Judge what a child like Midge could learn concerning responsibility by taking a job and earning her own money.

Chapters 5 and 6

VOCABULARY:

platform
tip

KNOWLEDGE:

1. Where had Aunt Claudia met Al?
2. What was Sarah Ida's "apron"?
3. Who was Sarah's first customer?
4. What rule about shining shoes did Al most emphasize?
5. Where did Al get the new apron?

COMPREHENSION:

1. Explain why Kicker had never worked for Al.
2. Why was Sarah surprised that her aunt was allowing her to work for Al?
3. Explain why Al extended the girl's hours to a full day.
4. Why did Al become very angry with Sarah Ida?
5. Explain, as if you were Al, the best way to shine shoes. Prepare a list of items needed.
6. How did Al clear away the black shoe polish?

APPLICATION:

1. Find information about the custom of tipping. What percentage is considered correct, for example, in a restaurant?
2. Share "firsts." As a class, recall humorous experiences that you have had learning a new skill.
3. Demonstrate your reaction if the strange boy had silently watched you.
4. Tell the story from the point of view of the customer with the brown shoes.
5. Demonstrate Al's method of shining shoes for the class.
6. Interview Al to find out why he thought that being courteous was the most important rule.

ANALYSIS:

1. Read excerpts from *Oliver Twist* by Charles Dickens. Compare Oliver to Sarah Ida. How were they alike? Different?
2. As a class, discuss why polished shoes are considered a symbol of power in many parts of the world. Discuss other symbols of power.
3. Identify the portions of the chapter in which Sarah Ida was most scared, embarrassed, or proud.
4. Did Al treat his employee like a child or an adult? Compare your opinions with a partner.

SYNTHESIS:

1. Design an apron for the shoeshine stand. Devise a clever way to advertise on the front.
2. Read *The Eternal Spring of Mr. Ito* by Shela Garrigue. Draw a bonsai tree as the object that helped Sarah grow. Draw the object from *Shoeshine Girl* that helped Sarah Ida grow.
3. Create another mysterious character along with Kicker. Write a short mystery story involving Sarah Ida, Al, and Aunt Claudia.
4. An Indian saying tells us that we must walk in someone else's moccasins before we can understand them. Create a new adventure where you walk in a favorite character's moccasins. Examples could be Henry or Beezus from *Ramona the Pest* by Beverly Cleary. Share your written adventure with the class.
5. Realistic fiction portrays characters candidly. Which character from this book could join your class? Write about a day in your school with the character of your choice.

EVALUATION:

1. Judge whether Al should have helped Sarah Ida when she made a mistake with the black shoe polish. Why or why not?
2. Determine Sarah's first response to frustration. Does she think of the immediate or long-term results of her actions? Explain.
3. Think of the Peanuts characters. Which character's personality is similar to Sarah Ida's? Explain your opinion.
4. Determine your opinion of Kicker. Would you want him for an acquaintance or friend? Explain why or why not.
5. Judge what Al thought of Sarah's first attempts as a shoeshine girl. As Al, write a recommendation for a new job.
6. What is more important to Sarah Ida, the money that she makes or doing her job well? Discuss with a partner.

To Al:
For
Cooperation
and
Leadership

Chapters 7 and 8

VOCABULARY:
ambulance
mouth harp

KNOWLEDGE:
1. Tell what Al's father sold in the South.
2. How did the rain on the roof bring back Al's memories?
3. Where did Al and his father live?
4. State the reason that Al received a medal.
5. Recall what fell from Al's pocket after the accident.
6. What was the reaction of Al's class when he received a medal?

COMPREHENSION:
1. Explain why Sarah Ida went to Al's house.
2. How did Sarah Ida's desire to help Al overcome her desire to keep her earnings?
3. Why was Mrs. Winkler worried about Al's business after the accident?
4. How did Al's customers help Sarah Ida decide to keep the shoeshine stand open?
5. Explain why Al was taken to a hospital.

APPLICATION:
1. Recall Sarah Ida's reaction to seeing Al's medal. What could she have said that would have been more sensitive to Al's feelings?
2. Grandparents or older friends sometimes tell stories about their school days. Ask an older person about his or her education and share the responses with the class.
3. Compose questions and answers about the important events in the book. Divide the class into two teams to see who remembers more facts about the story.
4. Hold a press conference as Sarah Ida, witness to the accident. News reporters from around the city interview you. Remember the five Ws—who, what, when, why, and where.
5. Learn about the old-fashioned traveling medicine shows. Share the information with your class.
6. Al shared an important memory with Sarah Ida. Write a page for a journal about your most memorable childhood experience.

ANALYSIS:
1. Analyze Mrs. Winkler's thoughts when she was offered Sarah Ida's earnings.
2. Would you have liked to live as Al and his father did? Explain.
3. How was Al like his teacher concerning rewards?
4. Identify the event in the story that signified that Al was no longer a stranger.
5. How had the accident been a turning point in Sarah Ida's life? Explain.
6. How did the rain and its sound on the tin roof help Al and Sarah Ida become closer friends?
7. Although Al had only gone to school for six months, he was very wise. Find points in the story to prove this.
8. Analyze why an award that can be seen is often more meaningful to a person.

SYNTHESIS:
1. Make paper bag puppets. Recreate the events leading to Sarah Ida's change of attitude.
2. Create posters with rules of safety for children as pedestrians. Place the posters around your school.
3. Tape record a book review of *Shoeshine Girl* for the media center. Chapter 8 would adapt well due to the sound effects of the accident. Responses from the reporters and Mrs. Winkler could add additional interest.
4. Imagine a conversation between you and Al immediately following the accident. What would you have said to make him feel better? Role play with a partner.
5. Create a watercolor impression of Al and Sarah Ida's rainy day conversation.
6. Write a class newspaper. Summarize the reasons why you would recommend favorite books. Share with students in other classes.
7. Dressed as young Al, tell how you won your medal and why you will always value it.

EVALUATION:
1. Determine your feelings about Al's father. Do you think that he was responsible for Al's lack of education? Explain.
2. Judge ways that Al could expand his business through advertisement.
3. Could Al have been a successful teacher? Find points in the story to tell why or why not.
4. Judge what Sarah Ida's reaction to Al's accident would have been when she first arrived at Aunt Claudia's home.

Chapters 9 and 10

VOCABULARY:
famous
crick

KNOWLEDGE:
1. List two things that Sarah Ida did to make Al's customers more comfortable.
2. What headline was on the front page of the newspaper?
3. Who brought lunch to Sarah Ida?
4. Name the person that Sarah Ida had thought was a bully.
5. Where is Sarah Ida's mother?

COMPREHENSION:
1. Explain why Sarah Ida's parents want her to come home.
2. Recall two events that reflect Rossi's generosity.
3. Locate the part of the chapter that shows Aunt Claudia's respect for the girl.
4. Describe Sarah Ida's feelings when she was asked to come home.
5. Explain why not accepting the lampshade was a difficult decision for Sarah Ida.

APPLICATION:
1. Invite a news reporter or a political cartoonist to your class. Learn about the process of creating and publishing a news story or cartoon.

2. Sarah Ida learned ways to care for others by observing Al and Rossi. How will her new skills help her to develop a closer relationship with her parents?
3. Write a poem from Sarah Ida to Al about caring. Choose from several forms such as cinquain, haiku, or couplet.
4. What might Aunt Claudia and Al advise concerning the value of money and its effect upon relationships?
5. Sometimes, like Sarah Ida, we learn from other people rather than our parents. Share a lesson that you have learned from a special person outside your family.

ANALYSIS:
1. Would you rather have had Sarah Ida as a friend at the beginning of the story or at the end? Explain.
2. Adversity often draws people closer together. Find examples in the story to prove this statement.
3. Compare Sarah Ida's friendship with Midge before and after her summer at Aunt Claudia's.
4. Analyze Al's thoughts when he realized that his customers had given extra money to him.
5. Tell the story from Al's point of view on his first day back at work.
6. What incident led Al to think that Sarah Ida had asked his customers for extra money?

SYNTHESIS:
1. Create a Welcome Home sign for Sarah Ida. Write messages to tell her how much she has changed. Autograph the sign.
2. If you were Sarah Ida, what would be your most treasured memory of the summer? Recreate your memory in a watercolor or tempera painting.
3. Suppose that Rossi and Sarah Ida had decided to run away. Write a new chapter ending.
4. Read the Greek myth about Narcissus which describes the fate of an uncaring person. Write an original myth teaching the value of caring.
5. Write a riddle about the main characters or important events in the story. See if your class can guess the answers.
6. As Sarah Ida, write a letter to Al telling how you feel about your friendship and what you have learned from it.
7. When Sarah Ida returns to her home she will make some new friends. As Sarah Ida, write a list of qualifications for your new friends.
8. Role play a scene between Sarah Ida and her mother at the hospital. Show how responsible and caring that Sarah Ida has become.

EVALUATION:
1. If Al were your teacher for a day, what lessons would he consider important? Explain.
2. Judge who was the bravest character in *Shoeshine Girl*.
3. Decide whether Sarah Ida's parents should change the way they relate to their daughter. Share your opinions in a class discussion.
4. Evaluate and discuss the paradox experienced by the main character: as she assumed more responsibility, she gained more inner freedom.
5. Determine if Sarah Ida needs to stay longer with Al. Has she learned enough about a caring attitude to change her relationship at home?

6. Evaluate the quality of Sarah and Rossi's friendship. Will the relationship last beyond the summer? Explain.
7. Was the newspaper story a kind of "award" for Sarah Ida? Explain.
8. What was an inner risk that Sarah Ida would confront by returning to her home?

Chapter 11

VOCABULARY:
embarrassed
platform

KNOWLEDGE:
1. When did Al first see the letter?
2. Who will Al hire to work for him?
3. What special gift was in the package?
4. What item did Sarah Ida take from the shoeshine stand?
5. Who was at the bus station to say good-bye?

COMPREHENSION:
1. Explain why Al gave his medal away.
2. Describe your impression of Al's medal.
3. Why is it difficult for the girl to go home?
4. Offer a reason why Sarah Ida felt embarrassed when she asked for the apron.
5. Why did Sarah Ida want to wait until Monday to depart?

APPLICATION:
1. Al gave his medal to a friend. What would you give to a friend in remembrance of your friendship?
2. Make a list of jobs for Sarah Ida when she returns to her home. Include a job demanding increased responsibility.
3. What would you do to help a hospitalized parent? List five of the most helpful activities.

ANALYSIS:
1. Why had Al's medal changed from a piece of tin into one of Sarah Ida's most valuable treasures?
2. How does the author show that physical activity can often help emotional problems?
3. What business in Sarah Ida's hometown would best suit her abilities? Explain your choice.

SYNTHESIS:

1. Create a medal for Sarah Ida. Use a symbol that she would appreciate such as a tennis shoe. Write an inscription describing her achievements.
2. Create a fantasy story. Give Sarah Ida three wishes to help her parents. Share the story with the class.
3. Make three sections of paper backdrop scenery. Design the scenery for a performance depicting the beginning, middle, and end of the story.
4. Videotape important scenes from your class's favorite books. Invite parents to view the composite tape.
5. If you had been the main character in this book, how would you have shown your appreciation for the caring that you received? Share your ideas with a partner. Create a thank-you card.

EVALUATION:

1. Was the medal the most valuable thing that Al gave to Sarah Ida during the summer? Explain.
2. Did Al learn a lesson in the story? Determine his most valuable lesson.
3. Al had earned his medal by helping his teacher. What had Sarah Ida done to earn a medal?
4. Judge why the medal was highly valued by Sarah Ida.

Additional Activities

ART:

1. Using charcoal pencil, sketch each character in an activity typical of him or her. Caption each picture.
2. Rossi made a lampshade that looked like glass with the light coming through. Lightly sketch objects or scenes from the story. Cut and glue colored tissue paper to the sketches.

DRAMA:

1. View the video production of *Shoeshine Girl*. Find a movie critique in your newspaper. Follow the example to critique the video production. Compare class opinions.
2. Read the myth *Daedulus and Icarus*. Role play a conversation between Daedulus and Sarah Ida in which they debate the need to take advice from their elders.
3. The role of the newspaper in social commentary was mentioned in the story. Find appropriate political cartoons and role play for the class.

CREATIVE WRITING:

1. *Shoeshine Girl* is the story of a girl who took an unusual job for a female. Think of other instances when boys or girls can take unusual jobs. For example, a boy could start his own baby-sitting service. Write a story about the barriers and ultimate triumph of the main character.

2. Think of "what ifs" for the main characters as story starters. What if Al had never recovered? What if Rossi had been like Midge? What if Aunt Claudia had sent her niece home? Create an original story based on the story starters.

MUSIC:

1. Analyze some of the songs from the sound track of *Oliver*. Compare and contrast the lyrics to the feelings of Sarah Ida.

SOCIAL STUDIES:

1. Research the writings of Charles Dickens. What child labor laws did he help change? Find excerpts from *Oliver Twist* that described the abominable working conditions of English children.
2. Al was a mentor to Sarah Ida. Perhaps you can find a mentor who will welcome on-the-job observations. Share your observations with the class.
3. Invite an expert in shoe manufacturing or repair to your class. Compile a list of questions to ask. Create a booklet illustrating the facts that are learned.
4. Interview a stockbroker. Find out how stocks are bought and sold. Role play a day at the stock market.
5. Research to find out how coins are designed. Find out if past designs have changed. As a class, create a new design for future coins.

SCIENCE:

1. Sarah Ida's increased physical activity helped her to relax and think more clearly. Find information on the relationship between mental processes and physical activity. Make a list of appropriate exercises and activities for an inside play period.

Bulletin Board

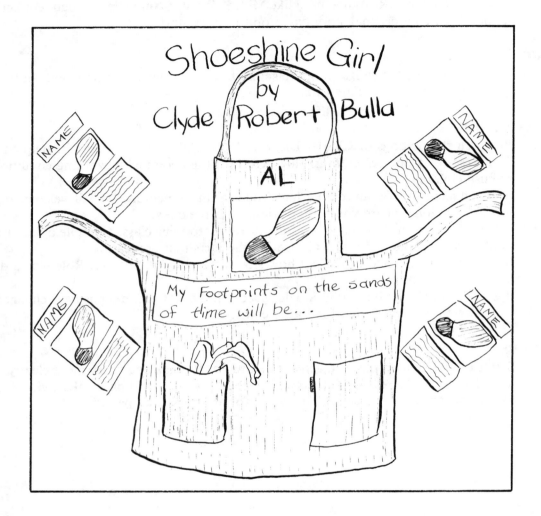

Create shoe prints on light paper. Outline the prints with a contrasting marker. Below each shoe print, students write a synopsis of what they hope to leave as their "footprints on the sands of time." Some students may want to create a new vaccine, invent a new space vehicle, etc. Display Al's synopsis in the center of the board. Each person's name can be centered above his or her writing.

The Mouse and the Motorcycle

by
Beverly Cleary

The Mouse and the Motorcycle

by

Beverly Cleary

On their way from Ohio to San Francisco, the Gridley family stops at an inn that is rather isolated from the main highway. Even though the inn is old and quiet, there are certainly adventures there.

Keith, the Gridley son, plays cars to amuse himself until he meets Ralph the mouse. He and Ralph are able to communicate instantly. This is an unusual feat for a human boy and a mouse. Both Ralph and Keith have a common love for a toy motorcycle.

Keith allows Ralph to ride the toy motorcycle and the adventures begin! Ralph wants to explore beyond his mouse hole home to other parts of the inn. Now he has transportation. His mother, however, has many fears about his venturing out beyond their safe home.

When Keith becomes ill, Ralph has to be brave and venture downstairs in search of the dreaded aspirin.

A lifelong friendship develops between the boy and this brave mouse that cannot be forgotten.

Chapters 1 through 5

VOCABULARY:

exhilarated   jauntily
antimacassar   momentum
relenting

KNOWLEDGE:
1. Who is Matt?
2. Relate four worries that Ralph's mother had.
3. What toy attracted Ralph?
4. Why did Ralph want children to stay in the rooms?

COMPREHENSION:
1. Describe how Ralph got into the wastebasket.
2. Why is the Gridley family in the old inn?
3. Explain what happened to Uncle Victor.
4. Why doesn't Ralph simply crawl out of the wastebasket?

APPLICATION:
1. Give examples for supporting *The Mouse and the Motorcycle* as being a book of fiction.
2. Demonstrate what you would do if you found a mouse in your wastebasket.
3. How would you get out of the wastebasket if you were Ralph?
4. Write a short paragraph about a magic meeting with an imaginary animal.

ANALYSIS:
1. Describe the interior of Mountain View Inn room 215.
2. List words that describe Ralph. Choose one that best describes him.
3. Read other stories where mice are characters that communicate. Make a list of the reasons you believe mice are chosen in literature.
4. Analyze the meaning of the statement "You have to make a noise.... These cars don't go unless you make a noise."

SYNTHESIS:
1. Imagine you are very small and in the bottom of a wastebasket. What would your thoughts be?
2. Predict what will happen to Ralph if Keith's mother reports to the management that there are mice in room 215.
3. What if the little terrier had been a cat? Could Ralph had escaped as easily?
4. Create a new vehicle that Ralph could ride. Draw a picture to show how he would travel through the inn.

EVALUATION:
1. Why do you think Keith hoped that there would be mice in room 215?
2. Will Matt be Ralph's friend? Explain.
3. Decide why it would be fun to have a talking mouse friend.
4. Do you think that Ralph will continue to explore? Why?

Chapters 6 through 10

VOCABULARY:

cowered	incredulous
bravado	boasting
indignant	agitated
chastened	oblivious

KNOWLEDGE:

1. How had Ralph learned expressions such as *scout's honor*?
2. Where did Ralph go when he escaped from the laundry basket?
3. What was Keith's gift to Ralph?
4. What is it that Ralph's mother is afraid he might run into if he goes out to see the world?

COMPREHENSION:

1. Describe what was distracting the maid from her vacuum cleaning?
2. Explain how Keith made Ralph feel better the morning after he lost the motorcycle.
3. What does *war on mice* mean?
4. Explain why Ralph feels terror at the end of chapter 6.

APPLICATION:

1. Using mime, take the vocabulary words and see if a classmate can determine which word you are portraying.
2. What is a saying that is similar to "All mice are timid" that is not always true?
3. How was Ralph feeling when Keith states he is not old enough to be trusted. Relate a similar experience you have had.
4. Relate an experience where you have felt lucky.

ANALYSIS:

1. Compare and contrast the fears of Ralph and those that Keith might have.
2. Analyze the meaning of Ralph's mother's statement, referring to Keith, "But he's a person."
3. Reason what the mice could do to escape from extermination.
4. Take an inventory of books or stories featuring mice that have been read by your classmates.

SYNTHESIS:
1. Imagine Ralph is a _____. What changes in the story can you relate?
2. Give directions how to make a sandwich or dish to a classmate. Have them give you the name.
3. Imagine Keith and Ralph are girls. How might this have changed the story?
4. Prepare a list of items that Keith could have used for Ralph's crash helmet.

EVALUATION:
1. How can you explain why Ralph was not satisfied to stay on the one floor of the inn, but had to see the outside world?
2. How do you think Ralph will get the much-needed aspirin?
3. Decide if Ralph is brave to go out into the inn in search of an aspirin for Keith. Give your reasons.
4. Conclude if the only thing the Gridley parents could do was just wait until morning to get the aspirin.

Chapters 11 through 13

VOCABULARY:

pilfering	ebbed
ventured	tendrils
peculiar	crucial
staunchly	

KNOWLEDGE:
1. What made Keith's father and mother realize he was really ill?
2. Why was Ralph's mother so frightened of the aspirin?
3. What happened to Aunt Adrienne?
4. Recall the obstacles Ralph had to overcome to get the aspirin to Keith.

COMPREHENSION:
1. Describe Ralph's relatives' reaction when he mentions going after the aspirin. Why?
2. How did Ralph get under the drinking glass?
3. Why did Ralph want Keith's sports car?
4. What happened to the motorcycle at the end of the book?

APPLICATION:
1. Explain about a time when you were ill or frightened. Share with a classmate.
2. Make a list of characteristics exhibited by Ralph under the two categories true mice characteristics and fictional mice characteristics.
3. Compare and contrast the reactions of Ralph's relatives.
4. Write six sentences on strips of paper that deal with the story. Put them in the correct order.

ANALYSIS:
1. Analyze how you and Keith are alike? Different?
2. Draw a maze using Ralph's route through the inn. Discover how to get him from Keith's room to the places in the search and back again.
3. Describe the interior of Ralph's home.
4. Compare Ralph's speech to a modern boy's speech.

SYNTHESIS:
1. Design a costume for Ralph to wear while he is riding his motorcycle.
2. Create a meal to be delivered to the home of Ralph and his family.
3. Role play an interview with Ralph as a guest on a talk show sharing his adventure.
4. Translate the feelings of Ralph and Keith as Keith leaves the inn.

EVALUATION:
1. Do you think Matt will help Ralph keep the motorcycle a secret? Give your reasons.
2. What do you like best about Ralph? Why?
3. What will be Keith's teacher's reaction to his composition? Why?
4. Evaluate why mice are used so often in stories.

Additional Activities

VISUAL ART:
1. Create a diorama of Ralph's home. Think of things you would expect to find.
2. Make a game using the game board on page 73. Place a statement in each square.

Example:

1. Ralph loses time looking for the aspirin—lose two turns.

2. Go ahead two spaces as Ralph escapes the terrier.

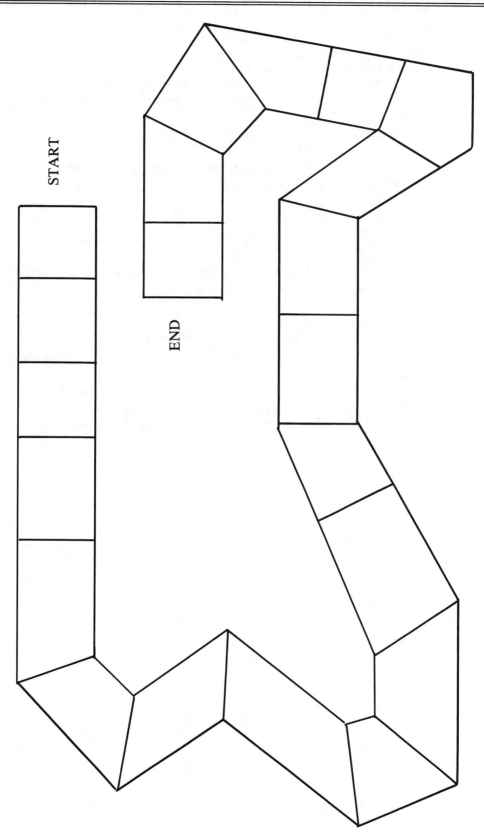

CREATIVE WRITING:
1. Write a summary of the story.
2. Write a short paragraph about the book describing the funny or suspenseful parts.
3. Write a pen pal letter from Ralph to Keith after Keith returns to school.
4. Write six sentences about the book that are not complete. Have the class complete the sentences. Compare writings.
5. Critique the reaction of people to mice. Write a letter to the editor of a newspaper expressing your point of view.
6. Discuss the components of a book of fiction. Have students make an outline of incidents that show action, conflict, and suspense.

DRAMA:
1. Record several sections of the book. Analyze what the voices should sound like to reflect the characters and story situations.
2. Have students practice storytelling. Have them dress as a character and tell the main events from that character's point of view.

SCIENCE/SOCIAL STUDIES:
1. List some needs that are common to both mice and humans.
2. Research science studies using mice. Discover why mice are often used in such studies and report the scientists' findings.
3. Project the story to the year 2055. Discuss what changes there would be in the characters, setting, and objects.
4. Imagine the story takes place in the year 1815. Discuss what changes there would be in the characters, setting, and story.

Bulletin Board

WHAT IF?

	Suggestion	Story
Ralph was a		
Keith was a		
The time was		
The motorcycle was		
Keith took Ralph home		

How would the story change?

1. Students write suggestions for story changes and place them in the bulletin board pockets.

2. Students choose a classmate's suggestion and write a short, creative story according to the changed character, incidents, etc.

3. Students share their rewritten stories.

Ramona the Pest

by
Beverly Cleary

Ramona the Pest

by

Beverly Cleary

Ramona the Pest is Beverly Cleary's tribute to Ramona Quimby, a kindergartner full of spirit. Her teacher, Miss Binney, describes her as bright, imaginative, but with problems getting along with her peers.

Each humorous chapter reflects the teacher's accurate assessment of Ramona. In the chapter "The Baddest Witch," Ramona's dream of becoming a Halloween witch materializes but with complications. As she becomes the witch, she notices that her peers do not recognize her. In her panic, she becomes afraid that she will totally lose her identity. Her solution is to make a sign with her name printed in large letters announcing who she is.

In "The Day Things Went Wrong," Ramona becomes a kindergarten dropout. She pulls Susan's beautiful *boing boing* curls due to her bossiness. Miss Binney, thoroughly frustrated with previous antics, tells Ramona to go home. What follows is a humorous but empathetic account of a child struggling with loss of self-esteem. Finally, after days of reassessing her relationship with her teacher and class, Ramona decides to try kindergarten again. Miss Binney can only hope that Ramona's desperate need for attention will not surface the moment she enters the classroom.

Chapters 1 and 2

VOCABULARY:
genuinely
rummaged
bluing
gopher
cotter pin

KNOWLEDGE:
1. Where did Ramona have to sit while the other children played?
2. What did Ramona like about Miss Binney?
3. Why did Ramona remain in her chair longer than the other children?
4. Recall what Ramona traded for the red ribbon.
5. Whose hair did Ramona pull?

COMPREHENSION:
1. Why was Ramona embarrassed to see Miss Binney on the second day?
2. How is the kindergarten setting important to the story?
3. Why was Miss Binney kind but firm on the first day?
4. What facts changed Ramona's idea about always having her own way in a group situation?
5. Find points in the story that indicate that Ramona would like to be older.

APPLICATION:
1. Read another book by Beverly Cleary listed in the front of *Ramona the Pest*. Think about the author's style. Write a letter to the author telling what you like about her style.
2. Have a nostalgic show and tell day. Bring a toy or game from early childhood. Make notes to tell why it is a treasured possession.
3. Ramona was puzzled about the words of the song that was sung in her class. Share class stories about words you misunderstood in kindergarten.
4. Howie was inventive and improved the tricycle. Brainstorm ways to improve common objects such as a student desk or playground equipment. Draw your design. You may find helpful hints about inventing in *Invention Book* by Steven Caney.

ANALYSIS:
1. Describe the relationship between Ramona and Howie.
2. Read *The Velveteen Rabbit* by Margery Williams. How was Ramona's rabbit like the velveteen rabbit? Bring notes for a class discussion.
3. Using stick figures typical of a kindergartner's drawings, illustrate what impressed Ramona most about her first day in kindergarten.
4. Pretend that you are Miss Binney. Describe to the principal how Ramona is different from the other children.
5. Observe kindergarten children on the playground. Compare and contrast them to the characters in *Ramona the Pest*. Discuss the likenesses and differences with your class.
6. Read "Invention" in *Where the Sidewalk Ends* by Shel Silverstein. Contrast Howie's improved tricycle to the invention in the poem.

SYNTHESIS:

1. Research the Caldecott books. Choose a favorite. Role play Ramona telling the picture story to her class.
2. As Beezus, write a short monologue telling Ramona about *your* first day in kindergarten.
3. Role play kindergarten interaction. Pretend that you are Miss Binney teaching a class about sharing. Ask the students to list rules about sharing. Ask why it is important. Teach an original game emphasizing sharing. Videotape.
4. Finger paint a picture of one of the humorous scenes from chapters 1 and 2.
5. Create a new version of a familiar fairy tale to tell to a kindergarten class in your school. Ask the children to help you create an original character or a cameo appearance of a favorite character from read-aloud stories.

EVALUATION:

1. Take a survey. Ask several students which Beverly Cleary books are their favorites and why. Compile the results on a bar graph.
2. What would be the quickest and most effective way for Ramona to become friends with Susan? Explain.
3. Was Mrs. Kemp's solution to the conflict about the ribbon wise? As a mother, what would you have done to be fair?
4. Using one adjective, determine the most outstanding personality trait of Ramona, Howie, Susan, and Davy.
5. Create a minicourt scene. Consider whether Ramona physically abused Susan and neglected her rabbit. Decide on a verdict.

Chapter 3

VOCABULARY:
 indignantly
 mysterious
 automatically

KNOWLEDGE:
 1. Why did Davy wear a black cape?
 2. Explain why Davy stayed away from Ramona.
 3. What was Ramona's first seat work assignment?
 4. Who was stuck in the chimney of the Quimby home?
 5. What animal did Ramona draw?

COMPREHENSION:
 1. What did Ramona's attempts at drawing the alphabet show about her personality?
 2. Explain why Miss Binney was indignant.
 3. Why was Ramona worried about Davy and Miss Binney's feelings?
 4. Recall why Ramona felt that writing her name was unfair.
 5. How did Ramona influence Davy's writing?

APPLICATION:
 1. Why do people like Ramona sometimes try so hard that they lose their friends? Discuss with a partner.
 2. Was Ramona the kind of student that you would want in your class? Explain.
 3. Ramona wanted recognition for her talent in drawing. Who has encouraged and recognized your talents? Share your talents in a special class talent show inviting those who have encouraged you.
 4. Ramona often compared herself to her older sister, Beezus. How can a child benefit from having an older brother or sister? Explain.

ANALYSIS:
 1. Read the poem "Jabberwocky" by Lewis Carroll. How was the author's attitude about words like Ramona's?
 2. Ramona struggled with fears. Analyze one of her fears and help find a solution.
 3. Identify an event in the story that could change Miss Binney's opinion of Ramona.

SYNTHESIS:
 1. As Santa Claus's attorney, write a letter to the Quimby family. Inform them why your client is bringing charges against them.
 2. Pretend that you are Susan, Howie, Davy, or Ramona. Write a real estate ad advertising your house for sale.
 3. Create an animal creature from each letter of the alphabet. Combine several, for characters in a fantasy story or folktale.
 4. As Ramona, you are a girl with few friends. Write a help wanted ad advertising for new friends.

EVALUATION:

1. Ramona became overly anxious about her seat work. List the most productive methods to complete assignments.
2. Judge whether Ramona will have a positive influence on Davy. Explain.
3. Determine which character has done the most original writing assignment.
4. Research the history of hieroglyphics and caligraphy. Determine which system that you like best. Practice writing your name using the system that you choose.

Chapter 4

VOCABULARY:

sensible	asphalt
peered	gouged

KNOWLEDGE:

1. Tell why Ramona hid behind the trash cans.
2. List two reasons why Miss Binney would be sorry for Ramona.
3. Which children discovered Ramona?
4. What did Ramona like about Miss Wilcox's assignment?
5. How did Ribsy annoy Ramona?

COMPREHENSION:

1. Explain why Ramona thought that the other kindergartners were disloyal.
2. Why was Ramona afraid of Henry Huggins?
3. How did Beezus treat Ramona?
4. Why did the principal calmly return Ramona to her class?
5. Describe Henry Huggins's duties as a traffic boy.

APPLICATION:

1. Why is it necessary for children to take responsibility for their actions as Ramona was forced to do?
2. What might Ramona advise other students to do to better adjust to a substitute teacher?
3. Read *Thirteen Ways to Sink a Sub* by Jamie Gilson. Think about the way Hobie and Ramona treated substitute teachers. Make a booklet compiled of courtesy tips for students who have a substitute.

ANALYSIS:

1. Research comedy and tragedy masks used in the Greek theater. Tell in which parts of the story Ramona would have worn a tragedy mask.
2. View excerpts from *Annie*. What parts of Ramona's personality were like that of the comic strip character?
3. Analyze Ramona's motivation in hiding. Was she courageous or irresponsible? Share your opinions.
4. Practice impromptu speeches based on themes from *Ramona the Pest*. Possible topics could be "The Ideal Substitute Teacher," "The Importance of First Impressions," or "Change, A Way to Grow."

SYNTHESIS:
1. Read "Kidnapped" in *A Light in the Attic* by Shel Silverstein. How was the kidnapped girl like Ramona? Write a poem about Ramona's fantasies of bravery.
2. Write a narrative from Ramona's point of view describing what she has learned about facing fear.
3. "Curiosity killed the cat" is a familiar expression. In *Ramona the Pest*, curiosity almost killed the dog. Write a new ending for chapter 4 about Ribsy's career as a spy.
4. Refer to *Poor Richard's Almanac* by Benjamin Franklin. Find proverbs that summarize action in *Ramona the Pest*. Write a fable based on one of the proverbs.

EVALUATION:
1. Did the author describe Ramona's reactions in the principal's office realistically? Explain.
2. View excerpts from children's comedies such as "The Little Rascals." Determine what activities of children are generally humorous to an audience.
3. Determine what was Ramona's most embarrassing moment in the day.
4. In problem solving information is necessary. Determine how accurate information could have prevented Ramona's confusion.
5. Judge Miss Wilcox's major personality flaw according to Ramona.

Chapter 5

VOCABULARY:
sensible
construction
executed

KNOWLEDGE:
1. What name did the shoe man give Ramona?
2. Why did Ramona hate Howie's boots?
3. What did Ramona use to create a ring?
4. Why does Ramona want to be engaged?
5. What warning did Henry Huggins give?

COMPREHENSION:
1. What mood does the author develop by describing Ramona's problem?
2. Explain why Ramona suddenly changed her mind about Henry Huggins after the rescue.
3. Identify words that describe Ramona's loyalty to Miss Binney.
4. Explain why Ramona wanted to use a tow truck during the rescue.
5. What was the motorist's opinion of Ramona's problem?

APPLICATION:
1. Read "The Bear and the Crow" in Arnold Lobel's *Fables*. What lesson does the bear learn that Ramona should learn?
2. As Henry Huggins, list student traffic rules for intersection crossings.

3. Miss Binney reacted calmly to Ramona's crisis. Share examples of when you acted calmly and cooly during a crisis.
4. If you had been trapped like Ramona, what would you have done?

ANALYSIS:
1. Ramona often seeks attention. What could she have done with the worm to gain positive attention? Explain.
2. Identify points in the story that indicate how Henry feels about Ramona.
3. Why was Miss Binney surprised at the seriousness of Ramona's problem?
4. How do the kindergartners encourage Ramona's teasing?

SYNTHESIS:
1. Create a "This Was Your Life, Ramona Quimby." Write a short script and role play Ramona dressed as an elderly woman. Friends and family appear to remind her of the most humorous episodes in the book.
2. Ramona needs a new invention to rescue her. Read *Henry Reed, Inc.* by Keith Robertson. Write a conversation between Ramona and Henry Reed about this new invention. Illustrate the invention.
3. Tell Ramona's engagement ring story from the worm's point of view.
4. Role play a scene with the school counselor in a group session. Cinderella and Ramona talk about the trauma of losing shoes and boots. Henry Huggins and the Prince relate their feelings about being rescuers. What does the counselor recommend?

EVALUATION:
1. Why is the description of Ramona's rescue humorous although it was potentially dangerous?
2. Judge how Ramona is like Henny Penny when she panics.
3. Determine what each of the following characters would have said upon hearing of Ramona's rescue: Mrs. Wilcox, Mrs. Quimby, and Beezus.
4. Predict what would have happened if Henry Huggins had refused to rescue Ramona.
5. What is Ramona's most positive personality trait?
6. Determine a unique way for Ramona to apologize to Henry Huggins and Miss Binney for the problems that she has caused.

Chapter 6

VOCABULARY:
muffled   stampeding
pantalette   supervising

KNOWLEDGE:
1. Recall why Howie was unhappy with his costume.
2. What did Ramona draw under her name?
3. Why did Ramona think that Ribsy recognized her?
4. How did Ramona want Howie to help her?
5. Recall what Ramona considered unrealistic about her witch's costume.

COMPREHENSION:
1. Locate the point in the story when Ramona first thought she was losing her identity.
2. Explain why Ramona wanted to impress her classmates.
3. Draw a picture of Susan's costume.
4. Why was the Halloween parade so important to Ramona?

APPLICATION:
1. Ramona was unhappy with her mask. What other costume would have fit her personality?
2. Think of a problem in which you can apply creative problem solving as Ramona did. Discuss.
3. Brainstorm a children's Halloween celebration. Decide on games, refreshments, and a costume theme.
4. Report on different holiday customs around the world. Report to the class on the most unusual.

ANALYSIS:
1. Why did Ramona suddenly pull Susan's hair and kiss Davy after resisting so long?
2. What part of the story indicates that Ramona had a problem distinguishing between fact and fantasy?
3. Contrast Ramona's personality when she felt no one knew her to her usual outgoing personality.
4. What emotion did Ramona express when she disobeyed Miss Binney?

SYNTHESIS:
1. Using paper, yarn, and markers, create an original "baddest" witch mask for Ramona.
2. Decorate cookies with designs representing characters in chapter 6 of *Ramona the Pest*. Examples might be Ramona's witch hat or Howie's cat mask.
3. Write a new episode with Ramona and her friends at a birthday party. Think of humorous problems for which Ramona can think of creative solutions.
4. Invite a theater costume designer to the class. Observe how the designer creates a costume from materials. Create a sketch of an original costume.

EVALUATION:
1. Judge if you think that Ramona and Susan's costumes were suggestive of their personalities. Explain.
2. Determine why people are generally less inhibited wearing masks.
3. Judge why it was so important to Ramona that her mother recognize her.
4. Determine how Ramona's solution to her dilemma was a compromise.
5. How was Ramona's response to the identity dilemma more productive than her previous responses to problems?
6. Judge Ramona's feelings due to her successful problem solving.

Chapter 7

VOCABULARY:
waggled
escorting
suspicious

KNOWLEDGE:
1. Who was finally going to pay a visit to Ramona?
2. What day did Ramona think it was when she became confused?
3. Who kept Ramona's tooth?
4. Why was Susan glad that Ramona was late?

COMPREHENSION:
1. Why did Ramona want to stay awake until very late?
2. Explain why Ramona was walking to school by herself.
3. Offer two reasons that Ramona thought that she was growing up.
4. Explain why Ramona was extremely angry when Susan called her a pest.
5. Predict what would have happened if Ramona had obeyed Miss Binney.

APPLICATION:
1. Tell about a time when you felt very strongly about an issue and were punished. Share with a partner.
2. If you were Ramona, what would be your plan to change your relationship with Miss Binney?
3. Ramona felt very lonely at home. Think of a simile or metaphor to describe her feelings.
4. Describe how Susan feels about Ramona's punishment.
5. Ramona just wanted to be forgotten or crossed out. Have you ever felt like this? Share with a partner.

ANALYSIS:
1. Explain why you think that Miss Binney's punishment was fair or unfair.
2. Analyze why acting big was the worst kindergarten crime.
3. Explain why Miss Binney uses the same punishment each time Ramona pulls Susan's hair.
4. Tell two reasons why Susan always tells Miss Binney when Ramona pulls her hair.

SYNTHESIS:
1. Draw Ramona's idea of the tooth fairy.
2. Mime a character from the story. See if classmates can guess the situation of the character.
3. Role play Ramona as a teenager. Interview her to see what humorous happenings have occurred in her life. Are Susan and Davy still her friends?

EVALUATION:
1. Judge what will happen if Ramona continues to disobey Miss Binney.
2. Determine if Ramona was really as alone and rejected as she felt. Explain your opinion.
3. Judge whether Ramona has finally learned a lesson due to Miss Binney's punishment.
4. Tell why removal from the group was particularly difficult for Ramona.
5. Determine how Ramona misinterpreted Miss Binney's meaning of brave.
6. Why did Ramona pretend that she could read Miss Binney's letter?
7. Judge whether you think Miss Binney's assessment of Ramona's behavior was accurate. Explain why or why not.
8. Who will Ramona's model be for future behavior? Explain.
9. Determine what you think will happen to the relationship between Ramona, Susan, Davy, and Howie during first grade?

Chapter 8

VOCABULARY:
negative
peer
truant

KNOWLEDGE:
1. Why did Mrs. Quimby have a conference with the teacher?
2. When did Miss Binney say that Ramona could come back to class?
3. What new name did Beezus give Ramona?
4. State how Ramona was rude to Mrs. Wisser.
5. Who delivered Miss Binney's letter?
6. What was the job of the school truant officer?
7. Why did Ramona want Howie to stay for lunch?

COMPREHENSION:
1. What did Mrs. Quimby think about Ramona's actions after her conference with the teacher?
2. How did Ramona feel about staying home after the second day?
3. Tell how Beezus and Henry influenced Ramona.
4. Explain why Mrs. Quimby allowed Ramona to remain at home.
5. How did Ramona compare kicking the wall to her previous actions?
6. Why was the *Q* in Miss Binney's letter particularly significant?
7. What happened after Ramona received her teacher's letter?

APPLICATION:
1. What could a child who is afraid to talk to the teacher learn from Ramona's experience?
2. How would you have helped Ramona return to her class?
3. Due to her experience, how do you think Ramona will react to future encounters with Susan?
4. Do you think Ramona would have had social problems in any class? Explain.

ANALYSIS:

1. Contrast Mrs. Quimby's attitude toward Ramona in the first chapter to her attitude in the last chapter. Has it changed?
2. What scared Ramona the most about staying at home?
3. Analyze Mr. Quimby's thoughts when he heard about Ramona's problems.
4. What incidents in the book lead you to think that Ramona is bright and imaginative?
5. Why will Miss Binney never forget Ramona?
6. What episodes in chapter 8 reflect Ramona's embarrassment?

SYNTHESIS:

1. Draw Ramona's face to summarize the events in chapter 8. Illustrate her feelings about the main events in the beginning, middle, and end of the chapter.
2. Ramona's Q cat has been through many adventures with her. Tape record an interview with her cat asking its opinion of Ramona.
3. As Ramona, write a letter to Miss Binney explaining why you have misbehaved and how you plan to change your actions.
4. Read "Snow White" to the class. Create a role for Ramona and role play her reactions to the familiar events.
5. Draw a humorous, sad, or surprising event when Ramona returned to her kindergarten class. Make up group stories about the various pictures.
6. Create individual cross-stitch samplers of the alphabet that Ramona learned. Her Q cat could be prominently accentuated.
7. Create a Beverly Cleary Night. Share excerpts from some of the favorite books of the class. Use storytelling and role plays for the presentation. Invite parents.
8. Choose emotional scenes from *Ramona the Pest*. Reenact the emotion and see if the students can tell the event that preceded and followed the emotion.
9. Create the lyrics to a song for Ramona. Refer to the lessons that she has learned and why she will or will not change.

EVALUATION:

1. Determine if you would want to be a kindergarten teacher. Why or why not?
2. Judge who you think was the wisest character in *Ramona the Pest*. Share your opinions.
3. Evaluate Mr. Quimby. How could he have helped Ramona?
4. Judge whether Ramona will be happy during the remainder of her kindergarten year. Explain.
5. Decide what you would have done as a kindergarten dropout. Explain in a class discussion.
6. Was Miss Binney more like Ramona or Susan? Did this affect her opinion of Ramona's actions?
7. Determine why it is important to judge a person's actions instead of their personality.
8. How could Beezus have been more sensitive to Ramona's feelings? Determine ways that she could have encouraged her sister.

Additional Activities

ART:

1. Make a slide projector from a cardboard box, rollers, and white paper. Illustrate and narrate a favorite chapter from *Ramona the Pest*.
2. Carve soap models of important objects from the book. An example would be Ramona's cat.
3. Create illustrations for invitations that Ramona would have designed. Send the cards to parents or to another class. Invite them to view your role plays from the books of Beverly Cleary.

CREATIVE WRITING:

1. Practice personification. Write a story told by the red ribbon. Tell how it felt to be argued about, twisted through wheel spokes, and, finally, discarded.
2. Summarize the plot of the story in one paragraph, one sentence, and, finally, one word.
3. Create a newspaper headline for each chapter of the book.
4. Read Rudyard Kipling's *Just So Stories*. Write an original myth or legend about the first alphabet.
5. Create a word search using the vocabulary words from the book.
6. Choose a character from the book most unlike you. Write a diamante showing the difference. (A diamante is a form of poem. See the appendix for formula and example.)

MUSIC:

1. Listen to a recording of "My Favorite Things." Write a new song based upon the favorite things of Ramona, Susan, and Howie.

SCIENCE:

1. Find information about pets and how they help children learn to take responsibility. What pet would have helped Ramona?
2. Invite an inventor to your class. Interview him or her to find out the process of inventing and marketing a product. Find additional information about the patenting process.
3. Thomas Edison was as inquisitive as Ramona. Find examples in a biography of how his childhood pranks helped him to become a famous inventor.

SOCIAL STUDIES:

1. Learn more about education in other countries. Research education in countries such as Russia and China. Determine how Ramona would have adapted to the educational system.
2. Research the life of famous teacher Annie Sullivan. Find out if her methods of discipline with Helen Keller were like Miss Binney's with Ramona.
3. Research the alphabets of various cultures. How did our alphabet develop and change? Share the information with the class.
4. Ramona had talent and an interest in visual art. Research to find out more about the first known drawings. Find examples of photographs of cave art.
5. Research folk and fairy tales from various countries. Explain how the different versions of the same story reflect the culture of the individual countries.
6. Read about Sequoyah. Report to the class how and why he invented the Cherokee alphabet.

Bulletin Board

Each child brings infant or early childhood photographs. Think of humorous captions for each. Under each photograph, the children write accounts of the funniest experiences that they had as infants or kindergartners. The teacher may choose to mount his or hers in the center.

Nothing's Fair in
Fifth Grade

by
Barthe DeClements

Nothing's Fair in Fifth Grade

by
Barthe DeClements

Nothing's Fair in Fifth Grade is a realistic account of Elsie Edwards and her inner growth during her fifth grade year.

Upon entering a new school, overweight Elsie is rejected by all of her classmates. To add to the complexity of the situation, she is found guilty of stealing money. An unforgettable turning point occurs when she tells Jenifer, a classmate, that she steals because she is hungry. She further reveals the depth of her problems concerning a neglectful and resentful mother.

Through the understanding and support of Jenifer and her friends, Elsie slowly changes. She not only loses weight but finds a productive outlet in math tutoring. Her school becomes an oasis for her.

Elsie's relationship with her mother continues to deteriorate. An alternative boarding school is used as a constant threat to frighten the girl. Finally Elsie is liberated when her teacher tells Mrs. Edwards that Elsie has improved more than any student.

Many lessons about family conflict and adjustment due to divorce are to be learned by reading this book. Perhaps the most important lesson Elsie learned is that physical appearance is relative and inner growth is possible even in the worst of circumstances.

Chapters 1 and 2

VOCABULARY:

gross   blubber

antics   latitude

longitude

KNOWLEDGE:

1. What did the students overhear Mrs. Edwards tell the teacher?
2. Explain why Elsie sat next to Jenifer.
3. What question did Jenifer's mother ask that surprised her?
4. Recall why Elsie must stay at home while her younger sister goes with her mother.

COMPREHENSION:

1. Describe Elsie's feelings when Mrs. Hanson scolded her for eating so much.
2. What was Elsie thinking when she pulled her own hair?
3. Why did Jenifer and Marianne suddenly change the subject when Elsie told about her mother and the sports car?
4. Explain why Elsie wanted to stand and watch instead of playing at recess and in P.E. class.

APPLICATION:

1. Write about a time when you were new in a school or neighborhood. Did a special person help you become acquainted? Explain.
2. Recall a time when you felt competitive with a brother or sister. How can Elsie's problem with her younger sister be resolved? Think of several solutions with a partner.
3. When someone is mistreated by a group but you want to remain friends, you face a dilemma. Decide on a positive plan of action.
4. Group action is often much different from individual action. Role play Elsie as your new next door neighbor. As Jenifer, you meet her alone. Would your first impression change?

ANALYSIS:

1. Read "The Ugly Duckling" and "Beauty and the Beast." How were the main characters' feelings like Elsie's? Explain.
2. Pretend that you are Mrs. Hanson in the teachers' lounge. Tell the other teachers about your new student, her mother, and your class's immediate response. Record the conversation.
3. Draw portraits of favorite characters from chapter 1 and 2. Hang the portraits in a gallery of favorite book characters.
4. What were Jenifer and Marianne's inner qualities that encouraged Elsie to disclose her fears?

SYNTHESIS:

1. Write a how to booklet for overweight and lonely children. List ways to solve their problems. Perhaps the title could be *Helping Hands*. Cut the pages in the shape of a hand.

2. Create a school lunch menu for Elsie. Make it nutritious and appealing. Design an award just for Elsie when she loses weight.
3. Write a telegram in Morse code or in an original code from Elsie to Dianne and Jack. Tell them of your feelings when they make fun of you.

EVALUATION:
1. Read about Ned in *Jelly Belly* by Robert Kimmel Smith. Judge how Ned's weight problem is similar to Elsie's.
2. Determine rules for a playground game that Elsie and the children can play in which there is no competition and everyone wins.
3. Why does Jenifer's mother think that Marianne has depth of character?

Chapters 3 and 4

VOCABULARY:

disaster	accused
swooshed	tattling
circumstantial	

KNOWLEDGE:
1. What did Elsie buy in the 7-11 store?
2. Why is Jenifer's kitten named D.D.?
3. What was Jenifer and Dianne's special classroom job?
4. Explain why Jenifer is relieved when the other girls talk to her about the class thief.

COMPREHENSION:
1. Explain why Jenifer was relieved that she had no birthday money in her purse.
2. Why does the principal describe the individual who admits taking the money as a strong person?
3. Why does Jenifer think that Elsie is the thief? Give three reasons.

APPLICATION:
1. What would Elsie have to do to convince you that she didn't take the money?
2. Read about Sherlock Holmes or Encyclopedia Brown. Adapt one of their methods to discover the classroom thief.
3. Who would you have shared your problems with if you had been Jenifer or Elsie? Explain your choice.

ANALYSIS:
1. Analyze how a Neighborhood Watch system works. How could such a plan work in Jenifer's classroom?
2. Decide why codes are valuable to detectives. How could a code help Jenifer and her classmates catch the thief?
3. Categorize the events in the story so far. Which are the most embarrassing, exciting, or funny?
4. What does Jenifer's father say that shows that he takes a comical view of her activities as a sleuth?

SYNTHESIS:

1. Fingerprints are used for identification. Using an ink pad, create a thumb or fingerprint character to illustrate a portion of *Nothing's Fair in Fifth Grade*.
2. Create a symbol for Jenifer, Elsie, and Mrs. Hanson that characterizes each of their personalities. Transfer your design to a T-shirt using fabric markers.
3. If you had confronted Elsie and she admitted stealing the money, what would you have done? Draw a one-panel cartoon using dialogue to illustrate.
4. Create a treasure hunt for your class. Hide something "valuable." Draw a map and connect the clues to find the treasure.
5. Design a Sorry, I Was Wrong card to Jenifer from Mrs. Hanson.

EVALUATION:

1. Compare the characters. Determine who is the most compassionate.
2. Determine the greatest changes in Elsie and Jenifer due to their classroom experience.
3. Judge your feelings about Mrs. Hanson. How could she have improved her methods in discovering the thief?
4. As a judge, explain the most important reason why circumstantial evidence will not convict a thief.

Chapters 5 and 6

VOCABULARY:

conference	sarcastic
allemande	probation
faculty	scrounge
lavatory	

KNOWLEDGE:

1. Who called Elsie's mother?
2. Recall why Jenifer had difficulty with fractions.
3. Identify the only student on the schoolground who cared about Elsie's feelings.
4. When did Elsie predict that Jenifer would stop being her friend?

COMPREHENSION:

1. Relate the story from Mr. Marshall's point of view.
2. Explain why Jenifer decided to become Elsie's friend.
3. Tell why Jenifer was very worried by the end of the day.
4. Explain how helping a friend in trouble can test the friendship.

APPLICATION:

1. Write a letter to Barthe DeClements. Find out why the story is so realistic.
2. Demonstrate what you would have done had you been as embarrassed as Elsie.
3. Jenifer was angry with Sharon because she criticized Elsie. Think of a time when you were critical of someone. Did learning more about the person change things? Discuss with a partner.
4. What has Jenifer learned from Marianne throughout the story? Explain.

ANALYSIS:
1. Describe how Elsie must have looked in the lavatory.
2. Tell why you would have liked or disliked hearing Elsie's emotional statements.
3. How was Elsie's life like an endless maze?
4. What did food represent to Elsie? Compare your opinion with a partner.

SYNTHESIS:
1. Choose a student in another class. Write a letter telling about your favorite part of the story.
2. Mrs. Edwards was poised like a missile. Illustrate this statement showing Mrs. Edwards as she must have looked.
3. Imagine that *Nothing's Fair in Fifth Grade* is a television production. Write a description for a "T.V. Guide."

EVALUATION:
1. Debate if Jenifer wants Elsie for a friend so she can help her with her math.
2. Judge whether Jenifer has really changed her opinion of Elsie. Find points in the story to prove your opinion.
3. Judge why the teacher asked Jenifer instead of Marianne to help Elsie in the lavatory.
4. Decide what would have happened to Elsie had Mrs. Hanson not sent someone to help her.
5. What is your most embarrassing experience at school? Discuss with a partner.
6. Judge what a school counselor would say to Elsie.
7. Determine why friendship is more necessary to Elsie than the food that she craves.

Chapters 7 and 8

VOCABULARY:
tangible
cancellation
decimals
nutrition

KNOWLEDGE:
1. Who did Jenifer tell that Elsie was her friend?
2. Why did Jenifer think that Elsie would use her tutoring money to repay the children?
3. Which student thought that Elsie had stolen the book club money?
4. Tell why Jenifer went to Elsie's house.

COMPREHENSION:
1. Explain why the children felt that Mrs. Hanson should have apologized to Elsie.
2. How did Jenifer discover that Elsie had an outstanding singing voice?
3. Explain why Kenny and Jenifer thought that Mrs. Edwards was mean.
4. Give three reasons why Jenifer wanted Elsie to tutor her.

APPLICATION:

1. How would you have found the money if you had been Mrs. Hanson?
2. Have you ever been wrongly accused? Write a paragraph explaining how you felt and how the situation was resolved.
3. If you were Elsie, how would you have felt being searched for the missing money?
4. Elsie discussed Mrs. Hanson's search and then pulled her own hair. As a friend, what could you have said to help her?

ANALYSIS:

1. Jenifer was confused about bringing Elsie home. What did she consider before making a decision?
2. Examine your feelings about Dianne. Do you think that she was justified in being angry with Jenifer? Explain.
3. What similar experiences had Dianne's mother and Elsie had?
4. Examine Dianne's change of attitude toward Jenifer. Analyze the reason for the change.

SYNTHESIS:

1. Dramatize the scene in the classroom when Mrs. Hanson discovered the missing money.
2. Think of another book in which Elsie could be a character. Write a new chapter including Elsie.
3. As Elsie, interview Mrs. Hanson. Think about the difference in your childhoods. Summarize by telling Jenifer what you learned.
4. Create a mystery story. Jenifer and Elsie are accidentally locked in the school at night. Footsteps approach....
5. A ballad is a narrative poem. Use facts about Elsie to write a ballad about her.
6. Create a bulletin board for *Nothing's Fair in Fifth Grade.* Draw important scenes and mount on a colorful background. Tell the story of each picture, predicting what will happen later in the story.

EVALUATION:

1. Determine if Jenifer's friendship will improve Elsie's feelings about herself.
2. Judge why most of the children are slow to accept Elsie.
3. Why does Mrs. Edwards seem to delight in blaming and punishing Elsie?
4. Kenny and Jenifer think that Mrs. Edwards is uncaring. Do you agree or disagree? Explain.

Chapters 9 and 10

VOCABULARY:
>   parole
>   sachets
>   altered
>   carbon

KNOWLEDGE:
1. List the items that Dianne's cousin shared.
2. State what Elsie's mother told her to do when she whined.
3. What did Elsie use to make her clothes fit better?
4. Who advised Elsie to become more helpful at home?

COMPREHENSION:
1. Explain why Mrs. Edwards screamed while talking on the telephone.
2. Why did Elsie's father stop writing to her?
3. How was Elsie able to provide gifts for the children?
4. Explain why Elsie started eating excessively after her parents' divorce.

APPLICATION:
1. Jenifer's mother had difficulty adjusting to her new job. Think of a family plan of shared responsibilities.
2. Make a babysitting pamphlet. List ways to entertain and/or educate a small child.
3. Elsie was resourceful in creating gifts. Demonstrate how to make an inexpensive but personal gift for a friend.
4. Create a composite picture of the girls in makeup at the slumber party.

ANALYSIS:
1. Analyze why the lavender sachet was a very special gift.
2. Why were Saturdays more fun for Jenifer after her mother started working? Explain.
3. Analyze Elsie and Jenifer's common problems with their brother and sister.
4. Describe Elsie when she arrived at the slumber party and after an enjoyable evening. Explain the difference.

SYNTHESIS:
1. What if there had never been a slumber party? How else could Elsie's mother have found out that people were aware of her neglect? As Dianne's mother, write a news story exposing the truth about Elsie and her mother.
2. Illustrate a minifamily photograph album. Include Elsie and her family before, during, and after the divorce.
3. Create a super hero or heroine reaching their goals based on themes from the book. Examples are an overweight person who finally excels in a sport, a father who gives babysitting lessons, or a student poor in math skills who finally starts his or her own business. Write a story about your super hero or heroine.

EVALUATION:
1. Which of Elsie's inner qualities aided her during a crisis?
2. Judge whether Elsie followed the old saying "Beauty is as beauty does." Compare your opinions with a partner.
3. Determine why Elsie felt that money wasn't important when she tutored Dianne.

Chapters 11 and 12

VOCABULARY:

snickered   admittance
lurched   lumbered
swish

KNOWLEDGE:
1. Who asked the truck driver to stop?
2. Give a reason why signaling to a car would not help.
3. Recall Elsie's plan of escape.
4. Who talked sympathetically to Mrs. Edwards?

COMPREHENSION:
1. Explain why Elsie was afraid for her mother to find out about her sister's "kidnapping."
2. Retell the story from the point of view of the waiter in the tavern.
3. Explain why Robyn remained in the truck.
4. Give a reason why the children were hitchhiking.

APPLICATION:
1. As Elsie, what would you have done if the truck driver had admitted kidnapping Robyn?
2. Think of a plan to write a license number if you had no pencil or paper. Demonstrate.
3. Formulate and explain an unusual and safe escape plan for the children.
4. Interview Robyn to find out how she really feels about her mother and sister.

ANALYSIS:
1. Why was the children's method of escape potentially dangerous?
2. Analyze points in the story that prove that Elsie is a responsible person.
3. Contrast an ideal mother's reactions to the rescue to that of Elsie's mother.
4. How were Jenifer's feelings similar about Elsie and D.D.?

SYNTHESIS:
1. Write a thank-you note from Mrs. Edwards to the tavern owner, the policeman, or the truck driver. Design the front of the cards for each individual.
2. In realistic fiction the setting seems real. Think of other settings for the chapters "Hitch-hikers" and "Outcast." Tell how the new settings would have changed the story.
3. Elsie, as a leading character in this realistic story, had many problems. If you created a similar story, what would be the leading character's main problem? Share your story with the class.
4. Collect objects that were meaningful to Elsie such as a safety pin, a piece of licorice, scales, or a note from her teacher. As Elsie and from your point of view, explain the significance of each. Videotape.

EVALUATION:
1. Debate the question of Elsie's guilt in not being more responsible for her sister's safety. Role play with judge, attorneys, and witnesses. Decide on a verdict.
2. Judge the reason that Dianne never discussed her involvement in stopping the truck.
3. Barthe DeClements dedicated this book to her son. How would you determine to whom you would dedicate a book?
4. Why isn't Elsie's mother more positive toward her even when she tries to change?

Chapters 13 and 14

VOCABULARY:
prejudice
crocheting
davenport
crouched

KNOWLEDGE:
1. What did the sixth grade boys call Elsie?
2. Which boy teased the three girls?
3. Why was the truck driver going to Snohomish?
4. When will Elsie leave for boarding school?

COMPREHENSION:
1. Explain why Jenifer held Elsie's hand.
2. Why was Jenifer's mother unsuccessful in changing Mrs. Edward's mind?
3. Recall why Elsie's mother had given up on her.
4. Explain why Jenifer no longer called Elsie a thief.
5. Recall why the truck driver took a long route to the shopping center.

APPLICATION:

1. Demonstrate what you would have done if the sixth grade boys had teased you.
2. Mime a presentation of prejudice in a historical event. See if the class can guess the event.
3. Think of a unique way to communicate to Mrs. Edwards that Elsie has improved.
4. Elsie's mother will not listen to her problems. Can you think of a method to encourage parents to listen more to their children?

ANALYSIS:

1. Did the children exaggerate when they thought that the truck driver was a kidnapper? Give a reason why or why not.
2. Contrast Dianne and Jenifer's mothers' conversational skills. Why was Jenifer's mother more skillful?
3. Dianne's attitude toward Mrs. Edwards was negative, while Jenifer's was more positive. Analyze the difference.
4. Why was Mrs. Edwards hostile toward people who wanted to give her advice?

SYNTHESIS:

1. Design a crossword puzzle using significant words from the story. Perhaps you can use words that describe the main characters or vocabulary words.
2. Tape record the conversation between Elsie and Jenifer as they both admit defeat. Role play as if you are angry, then nervous, and, finally, resigned.
3. Write a diamante (see the appendix) showing how Jenifer's feelings have changed toward Elsie. The title could be "Prejudice."

EVALUATION:

1. Elsie is passive with her mother. Discuss how her life would have been different if she had been more forceful.
2. Decide how Elsie's mother was like the mother in "Hansel and Gretel." Write a cinquain (see the appendix) showing the likeness.
3. Judge whether Elsie would be happier at a boarding school away from her mother.
4. Decide how a character from another book could have changed Mrs. Edward's mind. Discuss in a group or role play a scene with a cameo appearance by your character. For example, what would Ramona Quimby, from *Ramona the Pest* by Beverly Cleary, have said to Mrs. Edwards?
5. Determine why Elsie has a totally different personality around her friends as compared to when she is with her mother.

Chapters 15 and 16

VOCABULARY:
brainstorm
exemplary
pageant

KNOWLEDGE:
1. What did Elsie wear that was made by her mother?
2. Name Jenifer and Elsie's favorite library books.
3. Why did Elsie hit Jack?
4. Where did Jenifer and Elsie stay until school was out?

COMPREHENSION:
1. How did Mrs. Hanson convince Mrs. Edwards to allow Elsie to remain at school?
2. Explain why Elsie stared at her shoes.
3. Give one reason why Jack did not report Elsie's involvement in the baseball accident.

APPLICATION:
1. Tell about the parent conference from Mrs. Edward's point of view.
2. List some of the achievements that you would like mentioned if your parents had a conference with your teacher.
3. Interview Elsie's doctor to find out his opinion of her problems.
4. If you were Elsie, what would you have done to stay out of trouble?

ANALYSIS:
1. Why is Mrs. Hanson tired of hearing her students complain of fairness?
2. What did Mrs. Hanson's wink mean to Jenifer?

SYNTHESIS:
1. Construct a mobile for Elsie's mother showing symbols of Elsie's achievements.
2. Ad-lib a conversation between Elsie's shoes. Talk about Elsie's weight loss and how it has positively affected your lives.
3. Write a job-wanted ad for a newspaper. Each main character can advertise his or her services as a child or as a future adult.
4. Plan an award ceremony. As Mrs. Hanson, create a blue ribbon and a symbol representing each of the main characters in your class. Present the awards with a short speech telling each child how he or she is special.
5. Using fringed burlap and felt, create a bookmark for your favorite character. Symbols or descriptive words could be used.
6. Illustrate the beginning, middle, and end of the book by sketching three pictures. Use wet pastel chalk on paper.

EVALUATION:

1. During a panel discussion, decide each of the following: (1) Which character did you feel learned the most and why? (2) What was the personality trait that you liked or disliked most of a character and why? (3) Why is *Nothing's Fair in Fifth Grade* an important book to read?
2. Find a current television or newspaper account of children with problems. As a class, use the news excerpt to begin a chain story similar to Elsie's. Record your group story.
3. Mrs. Edwards changed also. Determine how the friendship and care that Elsie received also helped her mother.
4. Determine what will happen to Elsie next year in school. Write about your opinion in an excerpt from Elsie's diary.
5. Judge why Mrs. Hanson will always remember this fifth grade class.
6. Decide if Elsie and her sister's relationship will change. Explain your opinion.

Additional Activities

ART:

1. Create a six-panel cartoon that retells the story from a favorite character's point of view. Use two panels for the beginning, two for the middle, and two for the end.
2. Retell the book visually for your media center. Illustrate important chapters with oversized or miniature characters holding the book or chapter title.

DRAMA:

1. Analyze two videotapes by contrasting the following: (1) Elsie and Mrs. Edwards arguing points of view without really listening to each other, and (2) Elsie and Mrs. Edwards presenting their points of view using active listening and paraphrasing. Discuss the difference in communication.
2. Act out Jenifer, Mrs. Hanson, or Elsie during important emotional episodes in the story. Follow with a class discussion determining why the character felt and reacted as she did.
3. Select one of the characters in the book. Select an animal and research its characteristics. Role play the character as the animal which characterizes it. See if the class can guess the character.

CREATIVE WRITING:

1. Write notes that Jenifer and Elsie might have exchanged at school. The notes will summarize the book by referring to the main events in the story.
2. Read *Tiger Eyes* by Judy Blume. Compare the problems of Elsie and Davy. Include both in a news story that shows their ultimate triumph even though they have lost their fathers.

MUSIC:

1. Locate songs about friendship. Analyze the lyrics to see if they apply to the friends in *Nothing's Fair in Fifth Grade*. Choose your favorite to share with your class or a fifth grade class. To introduce the book, tell how the lyrics celebrate friendship as described in the story.

SOCIAL STUDIES:

1. Discuss the power of group dynamics. Tell how Elsie's personal conflict affected everyone around her. Illustrate with a webbing design.
2. Based on information concerning group dynamics, find historical examples. Discuss how personal conflicts can even eventually cause wars such as the Civil War.
3. Discuss the meaning of prejudice. Analyze the reasons for it. Read excerpts from *The Diary of Anne Frank*. Tell how Elsie and Anne must have experienced some of the same feelings.
4. Find references to current international and national problems based on prejudice. Discuss how the children's solutions could be adapted to the problems.

SCIENCE:

1. Research information about domestic cats. Find out about the amazing senses of the animals. Report to the class.
2. D.D. was important to Jenifer. Research information about your pet's breed. Find out about its origin and characteristics. Make a poster summarizing the information for a class presentation.

Bulletin Board

Each student writes a diamante (see appendix) about major changes and growth in his or her life. Above each diamante display a before-and-after illustration showing the change.

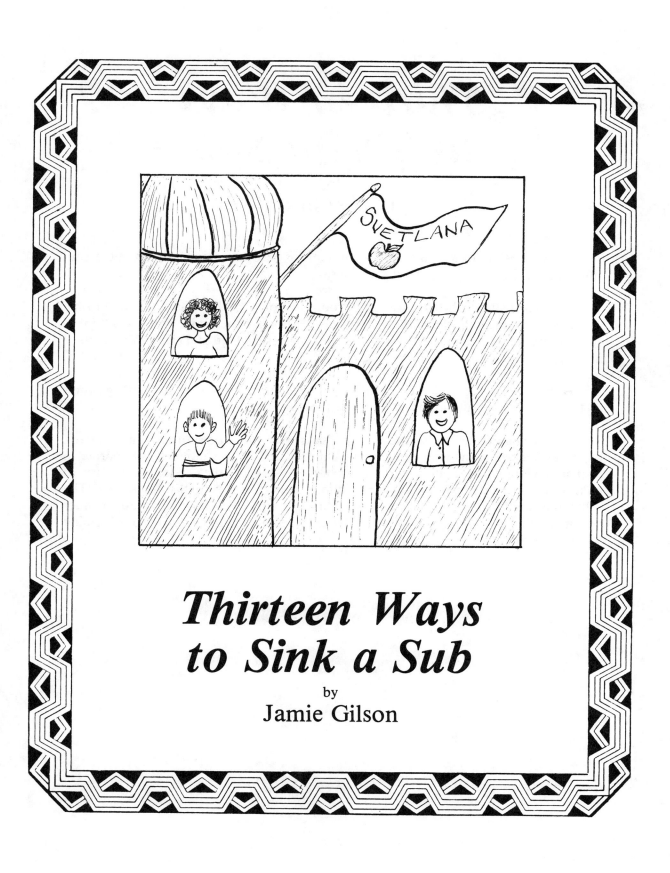

Thirteen Ways to Sink a Sub

by
Jamie Gilson

Thirteen Ways
to Sink a Sub

by
Jamie Gilson

Thirteen Ways to Sink a Sub is the humorous account of a disastrous but lesson-filled day in the life of a substitute teacher.

Svetlana Ivanovitch had expected a room full of good boys and girls due to her experience in teaching kindergarten students. However, the many pranks to "sink a sub" became almost too much for her. As she bounces back after each attempt to make her cry, the children become frustrated and, finally, amazed.

Hobie, the narrator, is the first to empathize with the teacher. His subtle gestures of friendship are finally modeled by all of the other children.

A final chapter describing the principal's discovery of a room filled with water and paper airplanes is a madcap climax. The children and Ms. Ivanovitch collaborate to turn an obvious disaster into a learning experience. Actually, the children have learned, unknowingly, a more important lesson about respect and empathy for adults. The substitute has learned a valuable lesson about group dynamics and her own inner resources. Together they have both experienced a very educational day—a day learning about life skills.

Chapters 1 and 2

VOCABULARY:

spectacular   polluted
squashing   kimona
villian

KNOWLEDGE:

1. Recall why Hobie left the rice candy at Molly's house.
2. Who was the Chinese philosopher that Hobie role played?
3. What was the name of the quiz show?
4. What was the deep purple cave?
5. Who owned the Chinese artifacts?
6. Where was the spit pit?

COMPREHENSION:

1. Tell the reasons why Molly felt that she was the leader of the class presentation.
2. Explain why the spit pit was aptly named.
3. How did Confucius and a game show host with a red bow tie find themselves together?
4. Explain why Nick was poking fun at Hobie's makeup.
5. Describe Mrs. Bosco's role in the social studies report.
6. Explain why eating rice was more effective than describing its taste.

APPLICATION:

1. Describe Hobie's appearance when he lost half of the mustache.
2. Have you ever experienced an anxious or humorous moment before or during a performance? Share with the class.
3. Create your own version of the Ting Tang show for a current social studies lesson. Invite another class.

ANALYSIS:

1. Identify a part of the story that indicates how Hobie feels about Molly.
2. Which episodes in chapter 1 and 2 are typical of a fourth grade class?
3. Identify the portion of the Chinese report that you would have liked to have presented.
4. Compare the words that Molly and Lisa used to describe the boys. Are they like words used in your classroom? Explain.
5. Why were the pointed tennis shoes significant to Hobie and Nick?
6. Analyze why the principal was reluctant to allow the children to enter the school building.

SYNTHESIS:

1. Illustrate with cut or torn paper silhouettes the most humorous part of chapter 2.
2. Read *The Eternal Spring of Mr. Ito* by Sheila Garrigue. Illustrate a picture of Mr. Ito's cave. Draw a second picture illustrating Hobie's cave. Title each picture, symbolizing the meaning of the caves.
4. Pretend that you are a talent scout. Ask the character who you feel has star potential to reenact his role in the Ting Tang show.

5. Design an oral game review. Divide into teams to research various aspects of the Chinese culture: eating customs, major cities, philosophers, etc. Adapt your review to Molly's format.
6. Create paper and fabric cutouts of the four children dressed for the Chinese presentation. Show them holding *Thirteen Ways to Sink a Sub*. Display in the media center.
7. Find examples of Chinese paintings. Create similar pictures using pen and ink or black markers on rice paper.
8. Create an oriental fan. Write a haiku (see appendix) about nature on the front. Exchange with a friend.
9. Create a composite design. First use the colors and lines that represent historical China. Later apply the colors and lines of the People's Republic of China.

EVALUATION:
1. Judge what Hobie admired most about Michelle.
2. Determine which of the children seems most serious about the presentation.
3. Determine why Hobie called Molly's grandmother the Danger Stranger.
4. What could the children have added to their presentation to have made it more interesting or realistic?
5. Determine why Molly discouraged her grandmother from coming to school.
6. What saying would Confucius have written about the Chinese presentation?
7. Which of the children's presentations reflected the most planning and preparation time?
8. Does the presence of adults affect a performance? Explain.
9. Judge why the boys made jokes before the presentation while the girls were determined and serious.
10. Judge why Mrs. Bosco might have special interest in the success of the children's presentation.
11. Judge why the children considered going into the spit pit the worst punishment.

Chapters 3 and 4

VOCABULARY:

inscrutable	mallet
Yangtze	Confucius
lunar	certified

KNOWLEDGE:
1. Describe Mrs. Bosco as she watched the classroom presentation.
2. Why did Hobie's face ache?
3. What did Molly use to get the attention of the class?
4. Name the country where Svetlana's parents were born.
5. What name did Molly assume?
6. Recall why Svetlana wore a foreign dress.
7. Who thought of the idea of sinking a sub?
8. What prizes had Molly and Hobie provided for the students?

COMPREHENSION:
1. Explain why the teacher was at the very bottom of the substitute pool.
2. Why did the children feel that this was their only chance to sink a sub?
3. Describe Nick's escape plan for Hobie, R.X., and Marshall.
4. Why did the students feel like kindergarten children after Svetlana talked to them?
5. Explain what the losers punishment would be.
6. Why did Hobie begin to feel a little sorry for the substitute?
7. Define what the children meant by "sinking a sub."

APPLICATION:
1. Describe the parts of the presentation that could be adapted for a book report.
2. Explain how the golden rule of Confucius could have been applied to the children's treatment of the substitute.
3. Research Chinese history to find out about other firsts besides gunpowder and paper. Share the information with your class.
4. What advice would you have given the children when they decided to sink a sub?
5. Would you want Svetlana for a substitute teacher? Explain.
6. How can students have a responsible outlook for class actions when the majority is acting irresponsibly? Discuss.

ANALYSIS:
1. Recall Svetlana's cultural background. How could she have added a personal viewpoint to the social studies presentation?
2. Tell the underlying motive for taking advantage of the substitute.
3. Why did sinking a sub suddenly seem like a bad idea when Svetlana explained her position in the substitute pool?
4. Read *Nothing's Fair in Fifth Grade* by Barthe DeClements. Contrast Svetlana's style of teaching to Mrs. Hanson's.
5. Why are Nick, Hobie, and Molly assuming leadership roles in the student plan?
6. How did the substitute turn the mispronouncing of Pfutzenreuter into a humorous moment?
7. What would Svetlana's reaction have been if she had known the children's plan?

SYNTHESIS:
1. Caricature exaggerates a person's facial features and dress. Draw a caricature of Svetlana Ivanovitch as Hobie would have drawn her. Include unique features such as the thick eyebrows and bell earrings.
2. Practice ad-lib and personification. What would one side of the mustache have said to the other? What would the green cave say to the purple cave?
3. Create a rice paper scroll telling the major events of chapters 3 and 4.
4. Mime different characters from chapters 1 through 4. See if classmates can guess the character.
5. Collect a sack of objects used in the story. A fake mustache, a box of rice, and a tennis shoe could be used. Write an adventure using any two of the items.
6. Find examples of Chinese writing. Write your name using the characters.

EVALUATION:
1. Judge why Hobie felt that it was important to impress Mr. Star.
2. Do you feel Mrs. Bosco was rude or enthusiastic? Explain.
3. Was Molly happy about the presentation? Explain.
4. Mr. Star said *friends*, but he meant for the class to listen. How did Hobie know the difference? Explain.
5. Describe two things in Svetlana's background that made her especially vulnerable to fourth grade students.
6. Determine how you would feel about grandparents watching your social studies presentation.
7. Which child is most enthused about sinking a sub?

Chapters 5 and 6

VOCABULARY:

fragile	origami
psychiatrist	fungus
hibernating	mostaccioli

KNOWLEDGE:
1. Where did Hobie, R.X., Nick, and Marshall hide?
2. Why did Hobie's mother always turn his pockets inside out?
3. Give two reasons why the substitute would not believe Marshall was Japanese.
4. What was Trevor's plan?
5. What name was Hobie afraid of being called if he became friends with the teacher?

COMPREHENSION:
1. How did Hobie feel about Miss Ivanovitch?
2. What did the clean chalkboard represent to the class?
3. Why did the substitute make sure that the children were watching when she slammed the snowball into the slide?
4. How did Svetlana demonstrate to Hobie that she had not given up?
5. What does Molly say that leads you to think that the sub will soon sink?
6. Explain why all of the boys wore the same watches.

APPLICATION:
1. Pretend that you are Miss Hutter. Advise a substitute teacher about teaching. Stress how you expect the children to behave and how to teach a social studies lesson.
2. Tell about the snowball incident from Svetlana's point of view.
3. The students displayed a type of courage when they tried to sink a sub. How could they have applied their courage in a more positive manner? Explain.
4. Make a booklet for substitute teachers. List activities that would be of a general interest for a fourth and fifth grade class.
5. What would you have done to change Molly's bossy attitude?

ANALYSIS:
1. View a filmstrip of "Rip Van Wrinkle." How was Svetlana like Ichabod Crane? Write a paragraph explaining.
2. Marshall created origami animals. Find out the significance of the paper crane. Explain why a gift of a paper crane would have been especially meaningful to the substitute teacher.
3. Analyze the humor of the Three Stooges. How was the episode in the teachers' lounge like their comedy routines?
4. Was the name on the chalkboard more rude than the other pranks? Explain your opinion.
5. What would the students say in a letter to their parents explaining their irresponsible behavior?
6. Should the substitute have given an ultimatum to the class? Why or why not?
7. What could the substitute have learned by observing Mrs. Franchini's class?

SYNTHESIS:
1. Create a snow scene using white chalk on blue paper. Under each picture write a description using similes and metaphors about the playground and how it must have looked.
2. Create a newspaper story concerning the snowball incident. Interview Svetlana and the children.
3. Write another adventure based upon your prediction of what will happen in chapter 7.
4. Create a design of Svetlana after coming in from the playground. What lines and colors would represent her feelings?
5. Role play a new version of the music class. Suppose that the children had played a prank on Mrs. Franchini. What might have occurred?

EVALUATION:
1. Judge why the boys felt that Marshall was more creative than competitive.
2. Determine what would have been an appropriate punishment if the boys had been found in the teachers' lounge.
3. As Hobie, write a note to a friend in another class. Evaluate how you feel about the plan so far.
4. Judge how the substitute displayed a sense of humor.
5. Is Miss Ivanovitch creative and resourceful? Explain your opinion.
6. Judge why the substitute chose Hobie for a friend.
7. Determine why Molly felt that the teacher was still scared.
8. Was Marshall interested in the children's plan? Find a point in the story to prove your opinion.

Chapters 7 and 8

VOCABULARY:

slogged	panicked
therapist	coax
prim	undisciplined
fangs	

KNOWLEDGE:
1. What did Molly add to Miss Ivanovitch's face on the chalkboard?
2. What did the substitute do with Marshall's paper crane?
3. Recall Mr. Star's first class assignment.
4. Who was the "artist" that designed Hobie's shirt?
5. What did Rolf drop in the radiator?
6. Who was Svetlana's partner for the Virginia reel?

COMPREHENSION:
1. Explain why the substitute genuinely enjoyed folk dancing.
2. Why did Molly say that violence was not part of the plan?
3. How do you know that R.X. is nervous about "Niagara Falls"?
4. Why did Rolf challenge the substitute?
5. Explain why Miss Ivanovitch was on the floor gasping for air.
6. How did R.X. try to convince the class that he was not responsible for his actions?
7. Why was it important for Miss Ivanovitch to draw earrings on the face? Compare your opinions with a partner.

ANALYSIS:
1. Did the substitute trust Hobie? Find a point in the story that proves your opinion.
2. What word would best describe Marshall when the substitute stuck the bird in her hair?
3. Read *Shoeshine Girl* by Clyde Robert Bulla. What advice would Al have given the substitute concerning rude and unruly children?
4. How was Lisa like the princess in "The Princess and the Pea"?
5. Why was it significant that Hobie felt like crying when Molly said that the teacher wouldn't come back?
6. Read "The Lion and the Mouse." How were Svetlana and Hobie like the lion and the mouse?
7. Why did Nick think that throwing paper towels on the ceiling would wipe out the mess? Explain.
8. Contrast the Virginia reel and Russian folk dances. How are they different?

APPLICATION:
1. What would you have done to teach R.X. and Molly to take responsibility for their actions? Explain.
2. Have you ever lost control of a situation? Share with a partner.
3. Invite a music teacher to teach a Russian folk song to the class.
4. As the substitute, apply your feelings to describing Molly. How would you picture a bossy and rude student?

5. Using Russian background music, such as *Swan Lake*, read a Russian folktale to the class.
6. Russians are famous for their skills in playing chess. Invite a chess expert to explain the rules of the game. Organize a chess tournament.
7. Svetlana evidenced her interest in American history by learning the Virginia reel. Learn a Russian folk dance and teach the class.
8. R.X. finally admitted that he had flooded the classroom and took responsibility for his actions. Relate a similar experience.

SYNTHESIS:
1. Rewrite chapter 7 as it would have occurred in a space capsule school. How would robots and humanoids change the story?
2. Can you think of a more creative way to have dealt with the substitute's injury? Explain.
3. As Svetlana, explain a parachute game that is noncompetitive.
4. R.X. flooded the empty classroom. What other pranks could the children have played while the class was gone?

EVALUATION:
1. What is the most believable reason that the children can give to the principal concerning the flooded classroom?
2. Judge the different teaching styles of Miss Ivanovitch and Ms. Lucid. Which would you have preferred and why?
3. Why was Svetlana intimidated by Molly's threat?
4. Determine Nick's feelings when he confronted R.X.
5. Judge why "Niagara Falls" was not considered humorous by the children.
6. Determine what R.X. did that signified a change of feelings toward the substitute.
7. How did Svetlana's Russian costume work to her disadvantage in disciplining the children?
8. Did Ms. Lucid consider Svetlana a child? Find a point in the story to prove your opinion.
9. Determine how the custodian will respond when he finds out about the flooded classroom.

Chapter 9

VOCABULARY:

custodian	sorcerer
apprentice	technical
chop suey	philosophy

KNOWLEDGE:
1. Where did the soggy paper towels fall?
2. What "science" lesson are the students learning?
3. Recall the fantasy that the substitute had concerning the students.
4. What had Michelle made in order to push the water into the bucket?
5. Who brought mops and buckets to the children?

6. Who told Miss Ivanovitch to return on Friday?
7. Recall why Mrs. Bosco brought fortune cookies and punch to the class.

COMPREHENSION:
1. Explain why Aretha came to the rescue of the substitute teacher.
2. Why were the students not upset at the possibility of the substitute's return?
3. Explain why Molly thinks that the girls have won.
4. What effect had a day with Svetlana had on the children's concept of substitute teachers?
5. Why was Miss Ivanovitch relieved that Molly wouldn't return?
6. How is the substitute's return a triumph for the students as well as the teacher?

APPLICATION:
1. Miss Ivanovitch will eventually have to tell the principal about the experiences of the day. Can you think of a positive way that she can describe the incidents?
2. Write about your own substitute teacher from a former grade. Share what was special about him or her.
3. If you had been the teacher, how would you have chosen ideal "substitute kids"?
4. Suppose that Svetlana Ivanovitch came to your class as a substitute teacher. How would your class react?
5. What did Molly learn from her experiences with the substitute?
6. Relate the chapter from the point of view of Mrs. Bosco.
7. How else might the principal have reacted when she discovered the flooded classroom?

ANALYSIS:
1. Listen to a recording of "The Sorcerer's Apprentice." How was the magic of the sorcerer more helpful than the children's elbow grease in cleaning up a flood? Explain.
2. Analyze the way that the sub finally sank. Was it the way that the students had expected? Explain.
3. Nick felt that the boys won fair and square. Debate his opinion with classmates.
4. What must Miss Hutter have thought when she entered the flooded room? Analyze her feelings.
5. Why was the teacher's manner more assertive with Molly?
6. What parts of the story made you feel empathetic with Svetlana?
7. Did this book deal realistically with current themes? Find points in the story to support your opinion.

SYNTHESIS:
1. Read *The Earth Is Flat and Other Great Mistakes* by Laurence Pringle. Find out the basic reasons why people make mistakes. Write a letter to Svetlana telling her why she made so many mistakes and how she could have corrected them.
2. As Mrs. Bosco, serve oriental tea and fortune cookies to the class. After the refreshments share fables that students have written based on the sayings of Confucius.
3. Create a picture of Miss Ivanovitch's fantasy class. Show the children glued to their chairs.
4. Write a letter of congratulations to the substitute teacher. Tell her why you think that she was strong, funny, and wise.

5. Role play Miss Ivanovitch and Miss Hutter's conversation in the hall.
6. Using colored markers and large drawing paper, illustrate the flooded classroom as it appeared filled with paper airplanes. For a dimensional effect, attach paper airplanes to the picture.
7. Find information about drawing cartoons. Note how eyebrows and mouths can change the entire facial expression. Draw a cartoon portrait of your favorite character.
8. What do you think happened when the teacher needed a substitute the following week? Write a humorous story about a new substitute from another country and the resulting chaos with Hobie's class.

EVALUATION:

1. Judge why Mrs. Bosco's attitude changed toward the substitute.
2. Do you think the children should have been required to clean the room? Why or why not?
3. During their day together who learned the most valuable lessons, the substitute or the children? Explain.
4. Judge whether you think Jamie Gilson's dedication is humorous. Explain why or why not.
5. Determine the best captions for the pictures throughout the book.

Additional Activities

ART:

1. Create a fabric banner to represent *Thirteen Ways to Sink a Sub*. Using yarn and felt, create a symbol for each of the main characters. Display in your school.
2. Learn about the Chinese art of paper cutting. Cut out a dove or snow-covered tree as described in the story.
3. Invite an origami expert to your class. Learn to fold some of Marshall's animals as well as more intricate shapes.
4. Create Kabuki masks. Using white paper draw the mask designs with black and red markers.

CREATIVE WRITING:

1. Research the meaning of the white origami dove in the Japanese culture. Fold a dove and write a message of hope on its wings.
2. Create a story about a Russian, Japanese, or Chinese student with an American substitute teacher. Relate the humorous events of a cultural mix-up.

DRAMA:

1. Using a puppet stage create paper puppets to reenact a favorite chapter from the book.
2. Invite another class who has also read this book to an impromptu storytelling session. Create stories for questions that your guests ask. For example, why did Svetlana wear bell earrings? Svetlana tells her story set in Russia. Another question could focus on why the Chinese invented gunpowder. As Confucius, tell a myth or legend about the invention.

SOCIAL STUDIES:

1. Create a kimono from fabric or paper using fabric or paper markers. Create a paper replica of modern Chinese apparel. Display.
2. Invite a resource person to the class to share slides of modern China. Interview for information about current political and social changes in the country.
3. Research and report on the significance of the Chinese New Year. Create a small paper dragon as part of the report.
4. Confucius wrote famous sayings. Ben Franklin also wrote famous sayings in *Poor Richard's Almanac*. Contrast and compare the writings of both men.
5. Read *The Master Puppeteer* by Katherine Paterson. Explain Bunraku theater to your class.
6. Find information and photographs of the Russian Faberge eggs. Share the information with the class.
7. Research Russian architecture. Create a display of onion dome buildings that could be found in Moscow.
8. Invite a theater makeup artist to demonstrate traditional Kabuki makeup. Turn a Japanese folktale into a play using Kabuki makeup.
9. Find sources for foreign pen pals. Choose a pen pal from one of the countries mentioned in the story, or other countries.
10. Ask a resource person to tell the history and significance of the Japanese tea ceremony. Role play an authentic tea ceremony.

MUSIC:

1. Listen to a recording or view a video production of *The Nutcracker Suite*. Analyze how the music tells the story.
2. View a video production of *Swan Lake*. Research information about famous Russian ballet stars and report to the class.

SCIENCE:

1. Research the laws of aerodynamics. With a paper airplane demonstrate flight laws.
2. Research Russian space achievements. Show a time line of their achievements.
3. Find out the components of gunpowder. Explain how they interact. Make a chart for the class.
4. Teach an eatable chemistry lesson. Research the nutritional value of the Oriental diet as compared to the American fast-food diet. Demonstrate the cooking of a simple Oriental dish such as tempura.
5. Research how the oyster produces a pearl. Learn how the Japanese produce cultured pearls in "farms."
6. Japan is surrounded by an ocean. Learn about the sharks and dolphins familiar to the culture. Find out why these sea animals are natural enemies. Report to the class.
7. Find out about rice farming in Japan and China. Why is the climate and land in these countries conducive to its growth?

Bulletin Board

Draw a T-shirt for the main characters. The background or lettering may be made of denim fabric. Each fabric or paper shirt is captioned with a saying symbolic of a character. Mount shirts as shown.

Bunnicula

by

Deborah Howe and James Howe

Bunnicula

by
Deborah Howe and James Howe

This is a story about a more than average family with two pets.

One night the family goes to a Dracula movie and discovers a small black and white bunny with a note attached to its neck in the theater. Feeling it had been abandoned even though no one could decipher the note, they take it home.

The dog and cat begin to be concerned as strange happenings occur. The rabbit, now named Bunnicula, can get out of his cage without opening the door and he has fangs as well as red glistening eyes.

Suddenly vegetables and fruits are white and without any juice in them. The animals suspect Bunnicula may actually be a vampire and attempt to protect the family.

Chapter 1

VOCABULARY:

manuscript	digress	decipher
obscure	bereaved	favoritism
Transylvania	admonition	tranquil
mongrel	dialect	moseyed
traumatized		

KNOWLEDGE:
1. What are the names of the two existing pets in the house of Mr. and Mrs. X?
2. Recall what scares Chester even more than the vacuum cleaner.
3. Which member of the family actually found the bundle?
4. When did Harold stay in Toby's room?
5. Explain who is telling the story.
6. What was the name both animals were called for a time?
7. What did Chester wish they had named the bunny?
8. What was another name given to the X family?

COMPREHENSION:
1. Interpret why the dog felt the three days before he was named were so stressful to him.
2. Cite the reasons why Harold didn't like going to the movies with the family.
3. Recall how the children named Bunnicula.
4. Explain why Harold could translate the note.

APPLICATION:
1. Locate the Carpathian Mountain region on a world map.
2. Look up and define some of the vocabulary words used in this chapter.
3. Develop dialogue between Harold and Chester about their lives.
4. Draw a picture of the little bundle in his shoebox.
5. Write a description of a time you brought a new pet home. What were the reactions of both family and other pets?

ANALYSIS:
1. Analyze the feelings Harold and Chester have to the new addition.
2. Read other stories such as *The Incredible Journey* by Sheila Burnford dealing with relationships between animals. Compare the similarities.
3. Describe Harold from Chester's point of view and vice versa.
4. Reflect on how the rabbit might have gotten to the theater and on the seat.

SYNTHESIS:
1. Design a new cage for the newest member of the family.
2. Create a name tag for the rabbit.
3. Write a newspaper article/advertisement regarding the finding of this deserted rabbit. Present it from the standpoint of trying to locate the rightful owner.
4. Predict whether or not this new addition will be an asset to the family. Explain your beliefs.

EVALUATION:
1. Do you feel Chester and Harold are happy? Explain.
2. Judge how Mr. and Mrs. Monroe fostered feelings of security in their family and pets.
3. Evaluate which character you like the best so far. Explain your opinion.

Chapters 2 and 3

VOCABULARY:

first edition	sustenance	exotic
disdain	fangs	energetic
idiotic	aura	vivid
cape	caravan	hideous
gypsy	pendulum	reverie

KNOWLEDGE:
1. How is Chester able to do a lot of his reading at night?
2. How did Chester get his name?
3. What book did Harold find "particularly delicious"?
4. How does one get a gypsy to tell his fortune?
5. About what time of day did Bunnicula usually awaken?
6. Recall why Chester couldn't reach the pendulum.
7. What was another word Harold offered in place of Chester's "challenge of the unknown"?
8. What unusual marks did the cat find on the tomato?

COMPREHENSION:
1. Explain how Chester arrived at the Monroe home.
2. Why was Harold feeling particularly neglected?
3. Relate the reason Chester protected his nose before swatting at the pendulum.
4. Why did Mr. Monroe wonder if Peter had his chemistry set in the kitchen?

APPLICATION:
1. Role play Chester explaining his discoveries and concerns to Harold.
2. Draw a picture of Chester sneaking up on the pendulum.
3. It would seem very incongruous to see a rabbit with fangs. Sketch some other familiar animals with new additions—fangs, wings, horns, scales, whiskers, etc.
4. Have you ever taken a bite of something only to have it taste completely different than you expected? Retell the experience to the class.

ANALYSIS:
1. Explain some of the reasons why Chester loves to read.
2. Relate why Chester is instinctively concerned about the rabbit.
3. Interpret Harold's reaction to Chester's story. Is he in agreement?
4. Analyze why Chester's choice of literature has helped him develop a vivid imagination.
5. Was the family overly concerned about the unusual appearance of a white tomato? Which character was?

SYNTHESIS:
1. Design an alarm to let them know when Bunnicula is getting out of his cage or into the refrigerator.
2. Create a picture cube using poster board or paper. Draw a picture of a key character on each of the six sides.
3. Change Chester into another animal that might find it easier to follow and spy on Bunnicula. Give reasons for your choice.

EVALUATION:
1. Judging from the given information, was Chester or Harold more intelligent? Present your reasons.
2. Debate the different theories about the appearance of a white tomato. Try to achieve a class consensus.
3. Discuss the differences within any group with the addition of another member. Cite examples of a new baby, pet, etc.

Chapter 4

VOCABULARY:

abide	feast
subtle	drooling
scholarly	sauntered
valiantly	zygodactyl
tropical	mimic
variegated	canines
oaf	zucchini
aghast	

KNOWLEDGE:
1. Why did Harold almost miss his meeting that night?
2. What was Harold's least favorite food? Why?
3. How did Bunnicula slip pass them?
4. Why did Chester feel Harold should watch his blood pressure?

COMPREHENSION:
1. Explain why Harold preferred staying in Toby's room rather than with Peter.
2. Recall Harold's actions that showed he wasn't in a mood to be subtle.
3. Describe Harold's relationship with words.
4. Why was Chester so disdainful of *Treasure Island*?

APPLICATION:
1. Research the differences between fangs and canines. List some animals that have each. Compare similarities.
2. Research some interesting facts about the area called Transylvania. Share with the class.
3. There is a variety of bat called a vampire bat. Report on it including the reason for its having this name.

ANALYSIS:
1. Analyze how Harold could be "smart but not the scholarly type."
2. As serious as the animals are in trying to solve the mystery of Bunnicula, discuss how they can seem so silly at the same time.
3. Distinguish between the factual information and the circumstantial they have so far.

SYNTHESIS:
1. Draw a picture to illustrate the section you like the most. Explain.
2. Haiku is a three-line poem that often deals with something in nature. It usually expresses a feeling or rather unique observation regarding its subject. Write one about the story.
3. Construct a mobile showing symbols of the important elements of the mystery.

EVALUATION:
1. Judge from the given information if the nature of a cat or dog seems to be more direct. Use the given text regarding investigating foreign objects and settling down to sleep.
2. Compare the conclusions the class is drawing at this point.
3. Predict what the next section will involve.

Chapters 5 and 6

VOCABULARY:

throttle	grimace	menacingly
dolt	emanated	immobile
shrivel	pathetic	blight
bared	hideous	inexplicable
pendant	verbalized	emits

KNOWLEDGE:
1. How was everyone rudely awakened?
2. What did Peter feel had caused the vegetables to whiten?
3. Explain what Chester had put all over the house to stop Bunnicula.
4. Why didn't Bunnicula leave his cage that night? Would it be the same the second night? Explain.

COMPREHENSION:
1. Why did Harold think Bunnicula had gotten Mr. Monroe?
2. Explain what Mrs. Monroe thought of Chester and his garlic escapade.
3. How did they know Bunnicula hadn't left his cage?
4. Why can they freely move and touch Bunnicula during the day without fear?

APPLICATION:
1. Review homonyms and associate that language lesson to a serious mistake Chester made. Show how other homonym errors could prove to be serious errors.
2. List at least fifteen words that you think directly relate to the story. Create a word search.
3. Write a poem or diamante using one of the following as a basis: Bunnicula and his unusual behaviors or Chester acting in his role as a private detective.
4. Draw a picture of Chester doing all his research.

ANALYSIS:
1. Discuss, as a class, some of the superstitions they have heard about vampires. Do these things correspond to what Chester has read?
2. Analyze why Harold was so hesitant to pick Bunnicula up.
3. Relate how all of Chester's plans backfired.

SYNTHESIS:
1. Design a vampire pendant with the required garlic on it.
2. Create a mime of Chester trying to imitate a vampire. Remember the natural characteristics of a cat.
3. Design a coat of arms for one of the following: Harold, Chester, or Bunnicula. Keep in mind the information regarding each you have read in the book.

EVALUATION:
1. Judge the snap conclusions the family arrives at to explain the unusual happenings. Compare these to ones you may have made only to change later when you discovered additional information.
2. Consider the story illustrations used in this section. Do you feel they are appropriate? Do they express the ideas, etc.?
3. Research Dracula and debate your attitudes about such beliefs. Discussion may include possible reasons for the origination of such folklore.

Chapters 7 through 9

VOCABULARY:

exemplary	devious
bygones	commotion
eminent	predicament
stealthily	hovered
scruff	fraught
trundled	sibling rivalry

KNOWLEDGE:

1. Explain Chester's exemplary behavior.
2. Why wouldn't the family let Harold play with Bunnicula?
3. What was Chester doing to Bunnicula that resulted in his becoming so ill?
4. What deadline did Harold have for Bunnicula getting some food?
5. Explain what happened to the food the children had left for him.

COMPREHENSION:

1. Define the term *sibling rivalry*. Relate it to something in either your family or another you know.
2. Explain why Harold only barks in extreme emergencies.
3. Relate how Harold knew Bunnicula was sick when the family hadn't even noticed.
4. What was Harold's rationale about why no one would notice if some of the salad vegetables turned white?
5. Explain the preparation a cat goes through to get into the attack position.

APPLICATION:

1. Predict the future relationships between the animals.
2. Make a diorama of the confrontations between Chester and Bunnicula.
3. Chart the positive and negative aspects of Chester's behavior towards Bunnicula. Do the same for Harold.

ANALYSIS:

1. Discuss how the doctor putting Bunnicula on carrot juice, etc., helped the basic problem.
2. Distinguish which sections of the story are unrealistic and explain your point of view.
3. How would your sympathies have changed if instead of the vampire being a bunny it had been a bat?

SYNTHESIS:

1. Create a dialogue between Chester and the cat psychiatrist. Chester is explaining the circumstances surrounding Bunnicula.
2. Design a different way for Bunnicula to sneak past Chester and get to the food.
3. Create a moral for this story.
4. Write a cinquain about one of the characters. A cinquain has five lines.

> Line 1 — name
> Line 2 — two adjectives
> Line 3 — three action words
> Line 4 — phrase about subjects activities
> Line 5 — another name for the subject given in line 1

EVALUATION:

1. Predict the course upon which the relationship between the animals will progress. Support your opinion.
2. Judge whether you believe Harold was a loyal friend to both Chester and Bunnicula.
3. Overall, would you consider this story to be basically positive or negative? Support your position.

Additional Activities

ART:
1. Design a poster warning people about the possibility of vampire rabbits—"Where there is one, there might be more!"
2. Using paints or pastels draw a picture of your favorite character or scene.
3. Create a coloring book about this story choosing the most important or humorous scenes.

DRAMA:
1. Give Bunnicula the ability to talk and create a monologue regarding the story or portion of it from his point of view.
2. Stage a mock trial with Bunnicula being tried for being a vampire. Review the criteria and legal attitude toward circumstantial evidence.
3. Using a play telephone be Mrs. Monroe talking to a friend about the unusual happenings at her house.

CREATIVE WRITING:
1. Write a translation of the letter found on Bunnicula explaining how and why he was deserted.
2. Alter the ending. What if Chester hadn't been so smart or the vegetable juice hadn't been effective? Write your new ending.
3. In place of minimizing his vampire background, heighten it with a story about Bunnicula going back to Transylvania to locate his *roots*. Give him some interesting adventures.
4. Write a sequel to the story which happens twenty years in the future.

MUSIC:
1. Compose a song or jingle explaining the unique talents of each animal.
2. Choose background music for each of the three animals, keeping in mind the unusual characteristics or talents of each.

SCIENCE:
1. Research the life cycle of a rabbit. If possible, get a rabbit as a class pet.
2. If it isn't feasible to obtain a rabbit for the class on a permanent basis, investigate the possibility of *renting* one from a local rabbit farm. Keep a journal of its behaviors including eating and sleeping patterns.
3. Develop a science acrostic by choosing a word illustrating a key animal character in the story. Arrange the letters down the left side of the paper and name some scientific fact or variety beginning with each letter.

Rabbits raised for meat and fur

Antelope jackrabbit

Blacktail jackrabbit

Brush rabbit

In Europe, rabbits are classified as *Old World* rabbits

Thickets are a favorite locale

Snowshoe hare

or

Belgian hare is really a rabbit

Unusual for mothers to feed kits more than a few weeks after birth

Nocturnal

Newborn babies are blind

In danger, a rabbit has been known to hop as fast as 18 miles per hour

Cottontail is a common variety

United States sports many varieties

Laboratories commonly use the Florida White

Arizona is a popular area for cottontails

SOCIAL STUDIES:
1. Using a world map locate areas in the world considered to be mysterious or the seat of unusual occurrences such as the Land of the Yeti, Loch Ness and Nessie, etc.
2. Look up and research the area known as the Carpathian Mountains which are located in Romania and Czechoslovakia. This area contains the region referred to as Transylvania. Learn about its history, dress, ethnic foods, customs, and folklore. If desired, research local superstitions. Share with class.

Bulletin Board

Have each student choose an animal a pet store might sell. They are to create a newspaper advertisement designed to convince children that it is *the* pet they would just love to own.

Crossword Puzzle

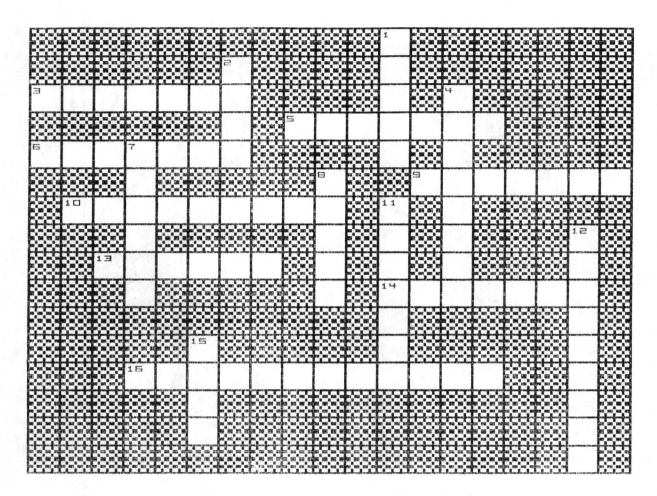

ACROSS CLUES

3. Country whose capital is Bucharest.
5. Mixed breed.
6. A type of bat.
9. Group speech variation.
10. Inquisitive.
13. Plant with red fruit.
14. People traveling together.
16. Area known for its vampire folklore.

DOWN CLUES

1. Canine teeth of a carnivorous animal.
2. Shoulder covering.
4. Translate strange written symbols.
7. "Little bird with a big mouth."
8. Nomadic person.
11. Movie the Monroe family saw that night.
12. Rabbit's name.
15. Enclosure.

WORD LIST: BUNNICULA

BUNNICULA   DIALECT   PARROT

CARAVAN   DRACULA   ROMANIA

CAPE   FANGS   TOMATO

CAGE   GYPSY   TRANSYLVANIA

CURIOSITY   MONGREL   VAMPIRE

DECIPHER

ANSWERS: BUNNICULA

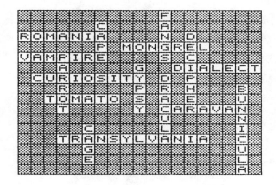

Be a Perfect Person in Just Three Days

by
Stephen Manes

Be a Perfect Person in Just Three Days

by

Stephen Manes

Milo Crinkley decided, by virtue of a falling book accidentally hitting him on the head, to become a perfect person. He was tired of his parents, teacher, etc., getting mad at him over things he had done incorrectly.

The book contained just three lessons, each one to be accomplished over a 24 hour period. Provided he could complete all three he would be perfect.

The first lesson is embarrassing for him but he is quite creative in explaining the reason he has a stalk of broccoli hanging around his neck. The next is a lesson in self-denial by only having water for an entire day. The last direction is the most difficult — not to do *anything* for 24 hours — not even sleep.

The biggest lesson Milo learned was about himself and his real strengths and needs.

Chapters 1 and 2

VOCABULARY:
perfection
essential
precisely
slurp
Venus flytrap
authority
smirk

KNOWLEDGE:
1. Define *perfection*.
2. What type of book was Milo originally intending to get at the library?
3. What does the K. stand for in Dr. K. Pinkerton Silverfish's name?
4. Recall the first lesson needed to become perfect.
5. Identify Milo's question that Dr. Silverfish immediately answered in lesson one.
6. Label Dr. Silverfish's unusual hobbies.
7. What was Milo instructed to wear to school on day one?
8. How did broccoli begin to take over his dreams?

COMPREHENSION:
1. Describe Milo's first encounter with Dr. Silverfish's book. What did that imply to Milo?
2. Explain why Milo decided the doctor was smarter than he looked.
3. Relate some of the experiences Milo had which helped him decide being perfect might prove to be a very good idea.
4. Recall how Milo felt being perfect would affect him in the classroom.
5. Identify where Dr. Silverfish is currently employed as well as where he obtained his degrees.

APPLICATION:
1. Using the description in the book, draw a picture of Dr. Silverfish.
2. List some of the qualities you think a person needs to be perfect. Share with class and create a class version.
3. Read aloud the section where Dr. Silverfish "knows what you're thinking." Be Dr. Silverfish.
4. Research some information about Venus flytraps. Report on their unusual qualities.

ANALYSIS:
1. Relate what was essential to becoming perfect. Explain how that same criteria would be effective in anyone's daily activities.
2. Explain why Milo didn't check ahead in the book for answers.
3. Interpret how Milo felt he fit into the family.
4. Analyze what Milo's first impression of Dr. Silverfish was and offer some possible reasons for it.

SYNTHESIS:
1. Design a book jacket for this book.
2. Continue activity 1 by writing a description of the author for the back flap of the book. Include the universities he attended, his awards and degrees, and some personal information.
3. Compose a poem on Being Perfect. Using your preference, make it either serious or humorous.

EVALUATION:
1. Evaluate Milo's attitude and concept of himself. Discuss the various answers given by the class.
2. Contrast the results of activity 1 with what you now believe Dr. Silverfish's attitude is towards himself.
3. Is it right for Milo to expect so much from himself?

Chapter 3

VOCABULARY:

contagious	snide
utmost	dawdled
astonishment	bullied
consumption	pungent

KNOWLEDGE:
1. What was the first fight of the day that Milo lost? The second?
2. Why was his sister glad he hadn't been given the part of the watermelon?
3. Explain what his mother wanted Milo to do with the broccoli after he got home from school. Could he do as she wanted? Why?
4. What was the one thing that Milo did at dinner which was absolutely perfect?

COMPREHENSION:
1. Explain why Milo preferred to dawdle before going to breakfast.
2. How did Milo explain the lumpy thing around his neck to his family?
3. Describe how the broccoli changed Milo's response to George's bullying.
4. Which class was the hardest for Milo that day? Explain your choice.

APPLICATION:
1. Rutabaga is the name of a vegetable many have heard about but not tried. Research the history and background of it. If possible, have a dish cooked containing some so the class can taste it.
2. List some of the reasons Milo gave for wearing his unusual necklace. Can you add to it?
3. Have the students predict what lesson two might involve.

ANALYSIS:

1. Analyze the reasons the story Milo told his parents differed from the classroom version.
2. Interpret his parents' attitude about the broccoli at dinner that night. Explain the reasons behind the difference in their attitude.
3. Create a new title for the book.
4. Discuss why Milo felt he needed to be perfect.

SYNTHESIS:

1. Sketch pictures of people wearing unusual vegetable necklaces.
2. Create a bookmark for this book including both the name and author.
3. People cover leaves with gold and wear them as necklaces and earrings. Brainstorm different ways to alter the broccoli so it would look more attractive as a necklace. Illustrate the best creations.

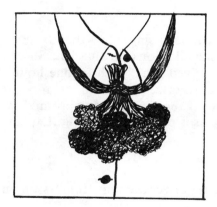

EVALUATION:

1. Judge whether or not Dr. Silverfish is indeed "perfect."
2. Evaluate what the relationship between George and Milo must have been before the broccoli.
3. Debate whether it is more important to be perfect or just to try.

Chapter 4

VOCABULARY:

wafted	humiliating
aromas	stoked
improvised	gurgles
scanned	trudged
peppier	feebly
rustle	fearless

KNOWLEDGE:
1. What did Dr. Silverfish's picture seem to be saying to Milo?
2. Tell Dr. Silverfish's well-known fact about humiliation.
3. How did the broccoli signify courage?
4. What was Milo's very favorite food?
5. Why didn't Milo tell his family what he was doing?
6. Explain why he waited an extra minute before looking at the next day's lesson.
7. What is the title of Dr. Silverfish's new book?

COMPREHENSION:
1. Relate how Dr. Silverfish's attitude changed toward broccoli in lesson two. Explain.
2. Do you feel Milo's father was supportive of him? Defend your position.
3. Interpret why Milo wouldn't have anything to fear the rest of his life.
4. Recall why television was a negative for him.

APPLICATION:
1. List some of the really embarrassing things that the doctor explained would never bother Milo again. Create some additions for that list. Share them as a class.
2. Watch television for a given time, such as one hour, and chart the number of food commercials you see. Categorize them as to fast food, soft drinks, candy, etc. Compare the class results and see if the time of day appeared to make any difference.
3. Research the term *fast* as it pertains to dieting. Explain why water is so vital while one is fasting.

ANALYSIS:
1. Analyze why, after the negative reactions from lesson one, Milo was so anxious to go on to the next lesson.
2. Interpret why, after just having dinner, Milo suddenly became very hungry. Relate how being told you can't do something can make you want to do that very thing.
3. Relate how Milo correlated the discomfort he had during the afternoon as proof of his broccoli story to his friends.
4. Have you ever found that aromas can create hunger?

SYNTHESIS:
1. Draw a picture of Milo and his excellent supper.
2. Make a literal illustration of one of the names the kids called Milo that morning.
3. Create a self-help tape on a particular need or concern.
4. Act out one of the two principal characters as if they were on a late night television program.

EVALUATION:
1. Judge how being so excited about doing something can actually make you afraid of it. Have the class cite examples of this from their own lives.
2. Evaluate how resisting temptation might help make you a better person.
3. Do you feel it's appropriate to comment on an individual's appearance? Explain.
4. Discuss why time seems to pass at different rates.
5. Judge whether or not we recognize individual differences at school.

Chapters 5 and 6

VOCABULARY:

dribble	fidgety
stick-to-it-iveness	vetoed
willpower	laryngitis
absentmindedly	solitaire
drowsy	kazoo
vegetate	obnoxious
hiccups	annoyed
brilliant	sly

KNOWLEDGE:
1. Explain why the next picture of Dr. Silverfish looked sly.
2. Give a synonym for *willpower*.
3. Recall his little joke about lesson three.
4. How did Milo know his father had read ahead in the book?
5. What do perfect people often do?
6. Elissa thought she was perfect. In what one area did Milo feel she might be right?
7. What occurrence a few weeks later gave Milo the idea he wasn't the only one interested in becoming perfect?

COMPREHENSION:
1. Define the term *willpower*. Tell of an incident where you exhibited some willpower.
2. Why did Milo feel it was useless to start over?
3. Explain how having the hiccups could make you less than perfect.
4. After it was all over, what were the three things Milo had been allowed to do?
5. How did his compliance show another quality he possessed?

APPLICATION:
1. Compose a class list of several important qualities, abilities, talents, etc., necessary for a person to be perfect.
2. List Milo's positive qualities.
3. Role play Milo after he had adjusted to not being perfect. Could this be done via mime?

ANALYSIS:
1. Analyze why his father became his strong ally.
2. Explain why Milo's mind was so active this particular night.
3. Think about what it would be like to really do absolutely nothing for 24 hours. Share opinions.
4. How did this whole experience make Milo happier with himself?

SYNTHESIS:
1. Design a Do Not Disturb sign for your room that is distinctively yours.
2. Create a picture of Milo in his room tonight.
3. Make a commercial for this book. Have it either recorded on videotape for television or as a radio spot.

4. Design a book cover for Dr. Silverfish's new book.
5. Create a moral for this book. Compare how this one might be different than one you would have created before completing the story.

EVALUATION:
1. Compare and contrast *doing nothing* to *bored*.
2. Judge why Milo began to question the wisdom of his need to be perfect.
3. Analyze why being perfect could prove to be negative.
4. Evaluate if you've known anyone who never does anything ill-advised or wrong. Is it really possible to be perfect?

Additional Activities

ART:
1. Vegetable prints can be fun to create. Potato cuts are most common but extend the activity to broccoli and cauliflower. Use your imagination to include other varieties.
2. Using the image the book presents of Dr. Silverfish as a base, alter it to depict him as a traditional businessman. Draw your interpretation of the result.
3. Draw a table centerpiece composed solely of vegetables.

DRAMA:
1. Role play a telephone conversation between Milo and Dr. Silverfish.
2. Do a monologue as Milo retelling his experiences.
3. Using an incident from your life, create a two-minute speech around the title "The Time I Was *Almost* Perfect...."

CREATIVE WRITING:
1. Create a picture booklet on "How to Be Perfect." Slant it towards the ridiculous or humorous.
2. Limericks are five-line verses usually rather humorous in nature. The rhyming pattern is first, second, and fifth, while third and fourth are together. Write one about the story.
3. Have Milo write a diary telling of the events of the last few days.

MUSIC:
1. Bring in different types of music and have the students listen to each selection. Evaluate how perfect each might be in expressing either a certain purpose or feeling. Possible choices might be:

1812 Overture	marches
Claire de Lune	Star Spangled Banner
waltzes	polkas
In the Hall of the Mountain King	

2. Compositions such as *Peter and the Wolf* illustrate how musical sound can express a story.
3. Have each student research and come up with a piece of music they feel is perfect for them. Take into consideration your basic personality. Lyrics may not be desired; the music conveys the feelings. It must extend to the different times and emotions you have: happy, excited, angry, sad, etc.

SCIENCE:
1. Get varied vegetable seeds. Plant them and keep a daily chart to see and compare the growth rates and development of each.
2. Examine and label the various parts of a piece of broccoli — flower, stem, etc.
3. Compare the internal veining pattern of a broccoli and a celery stalk. Use two containers with a different food color and water mixture in each. Cut the end off the stalk to create a clear vein end. Split the celery stalk part way up the stem. Place one side in each glass. Do the same with the broccoli. Over the next few days, watch the colored paths emerge. What does this signify about water pathways? Are both observations equally clear? If not, what are possible reasons for the differences?

SOCIAL STUDIES:
1. Discuss the term *perfect society*. Have the students research different people throughout history who felt they had the ability to create one. Report on each including their concept and goals, methods, and results both positive and negative. Compare and evaluate the results.

Bulletin Board

Each child is to either draw or bring a snapshot from home showing something very special to him or her. They are to write one or two paragraphs explaining the reason it is so special.

Crossword Puzzle

ACROSS CLUES

2. A type of turnip.
5. Milo's sister.
6. Perfect is _____.
11. The authority on being perfect.
13. Number of people in Milo's family.
15. Without mistakes.
16. First name of the doctor.
18. Where Milo looked for a book.
19. Dr. Silverfish had the world's second largest collection of these.
20. The first person who figured out what Milo was doing.
21. What Milo did which ruined his chance to be perfect.

DOWN CLUES

1. Sister's pet name for Milo.
3. Green leafy vegetable.
4. The name of the principal character.
7. Book—Make Four _____ Dollars by Next Thursday.
8. A person's life as described by another.
9. Dr. Silverfish's hobby is raising these.
10. He found his book in the scary _____ section.
12. Milo's father always told him; "don't _____ your soup."
14. The only thing Milo could have on the second day.
17. What Milo was allowed to do on the third day.

WORD LIST: BE A PERFECT PERSON

BILLION	FALL*ASLEEP	PEST
BIOGRAPHY	FOUR	PINKERTON
BORING	LIBRARY	RUTABAGA
BROCCOLI	MILO*CRINKLEY	SLURP
DR*SILVERFISH	MONSTERS	TOOTHPICKS
ELISSA	NOTHING	VENUS*FLYTRAPS
FATHER	PERFECT	WATER

ANSWERS: BE A PERFECT PERSON

Summer
of the Monkeys

by
Wilson Rawls

Summer
of the Monkeys

by

Wilson Rawls

Jay Berry Lee was a fourteen-year-old boy who lived in the vicinity of Tahlequah, Oklahoma, near the turn of the century.

He had planned an uneventful summer until he and Rowdy, his bluetick hound, discovered a tree full of monkeys. Jay Berry and Grandpa devised many plans to capture them and receive a sizable reward. The boy's dream of owning a pony and gun would then become a reality.

One comic adventure after another results as Jimbo, the most valuable monkey, matches wits with Grandpa and Jay Berry. A final attempt leads to research in the library concerning capturing the monkeys and the coconut *bait*. Foiling the elaborate plan leaves both the boy and his grandfather thoroughly frustrated and disappointed.

A flash flood has a dramatic effect upon the subsequent action of the story. It leaves Jimbo and the other monkeys cold, wet, and sick. Jay Berry discovers them and they finally follow him home to the comfort of the corncrib and barn.

The boy had always dreamed of owning a pony and a gun. Now his dream could materialize except for one problem. His twin sister, Daisy, needed costly surgery for her twisted leg.

A wish in the magic fairy ring and the subtle influence of Grandpa results in great sacrifice and inner reward. Jay Berry decides he must after all give his money to his sister. His inner conflict is finally resolved when Daisy returns from the hospital able to walk for the first time in her life. For Jay Berry, the summer of the monkeys would always be remembered as a time of development and change—a growing time.

Chapters 1 and 2

VOCABULARY:

bluetick hound	terrapin
land bottoms	pokeberry juice
sorghum	cultivator
jasper	katydid
sharecropper	slough
huckleberry	corn shucks
ramrod	turning plow
wiry	hopper

KNOWLEDGE:

1. What was the surprising offer in Grandpa's letter?
2. Why is one monkey worth such a large reward?
3. Define *bluetick hound*.
4. How was he always able to locate Sally Gooden?
5. What was his primary interest in the monkeys?

COMPREHENSION:

1. Explain the reasons for Jay Berry's special feeling for Rowdy.
2. Identify objects in the chapter that tell you of the time setting of the story.
3. Recall why Sally Gooden was a twin sister to the cow that jumped over the moon.
4. Why did people come from miles around to see Daisy's miracle?
5. Describe the family's first view of their homestead.
6. Explain why the monkeys were in the land bottoms.

APPLICATION:

1. Explain the differences in the way animals relate to Daisy versus Jay Berry.
2. Write a journal about your covered wagon trip from Missouri to Oklahoma.
3. Draw a floor plan of Daisy's playhouse.
4. Draw a picture of their new home.

ANALYSIS:

1. Analyze how the life in Missouri affected their feelings towards the new land and life in Oklahoma (sharecroppers versus landowner).
2. Explain Jay Berry's thoughts when Rowdy "bawled treed." Compare them to his thoughts when he first saw the monkey.
3. Contrast an afternoon of leisure in the Cherokee bottoms to modern city leisure. Explain which you prefer and why.
4. Compare Jay Berry's description of Grandpa inside and outside. Describe someone you know in the same manner.

SYNTHESIS:
1. Write a brief descriptive paragraph of a place you have seen. Use as many of your five senses as possible in the description.
2. Design an invention for trapping monkeys if you had been Jay Berry or Grandpa. Create a visual or oral advertisement for your invention.
3. Pretend that Jay Berry had been a city boy when he met the monkeys. How would this have changed the story? Explain in one paragraph.
4. Explain how you would create a crutch for someone if you were out in the wild.

EVALUATION:
1. Research *The Little House on the Prairie* books by Laura Ingalls Wilder. Compare the similarities and dissimilarities of their lives.
2. The story is told from Jay Berry's point of view. Do you think events would be related differently from his mother's viewpoint? Explain.
3. Who was the more imaginative child, Jay Berry or Daisy?
4. Decide what was the most unique personality trait of each of the main characters. Make notes about your opinions for a class discussion.
5. Judge whether you feel hunting animals is justified.

Chapters 3 and 4

VOCABULARY:

column	spindly
prowl	outsmarted
commotion	churring
eased	anvil
quavering	pertly
caper	squall
radiant	

KNOWLEDGE:
1. What was Jay Berry going to buy with the reward money?
2. What was Jay Berry's mama's attitude about trying to catch the monkeys?
3. What do boys and girls have to do for the old man of the mountains to like them?
4. When Jay Berry returned to his tree, all his traps and lunch where gone. Recall what happened.

COMPREHENSION:
1. Describe Daisy's old man of the mountains.
2. What frightened Jay Berry about the old man of the mountains?
3. Explain what it was that papa did not believe about the monkeys.
4. Discuss the action of the monkey that made Jay Berry angry.
5. Describe the hundred dollar monkey in Jay Berry's words.

APPLICATION:
1. Interpret bad luck spells. Share several bad luck omens you know.
2. Daisy had a way of making unbelievable things sound real. Demonstrate to the class an idea making it sound real.
3. How would you solve the problem of catching the monkeys?
4. Outline the steps needed to solve the problem. Share with the class.

ANALYSIS:
1. Compare how the old man of the mountains is similar to wild animals.
2. Calculate how much money Jay Berry could receive if he caught all the monkeys.
3. Identify the problems related to capturing the monkeys.
4. Design your vision of the area around the monkey tree. Create a maze for the class to enjoy.

SYNTHESIS:
1. Construct a mobile showing the raining monkeys.
2. Compose a song about something that makes you happy.
3. Meet with three classmates and discuss how you would solve the problem of catching the monkeys. Remember you are in the 1880s. Consider your capabilities.
4. Have the class break into groups to solve activity 3. Designate a reporter of the group to relate their solution to the class.

EVALUATION:
1. Assess Daisy's old man of the mountains. Do you believe there is really such a person?
2. Select three activities from the chapter that would not be done or seen today.
3. What does Daisy say happens to a boy who cusses before the age of twenty-one? In your opinion is this reasonable?

Chapters 5 and 6

VOCABULARY:
droning
hallow
lope

KNOWLEDGE:
1. What was it papa doubted the monkeys could do?
2. Where had Grandpa obtained the net contraption?
3. What animal did Jay Berry hate on the farm?
4. What did Jay Berry dread more than being hung by his heels from an oak tree?

COMPREHENSION:
1. Describe the night when papa and Jay Berry worked in the bottoms digging the hole trap.
2. Explain what changed mama's anger at Jay Berry to laughter after Gandy escaped.
3. Express Jay Berry's feelings as he related what happened to his monkey hunting.
4. What does Grandpa mean when he states "you know, it's always a good idea to have more than one iron in the fire"?

APPLICATION:
1. What would you have done if you had been chased by the monkeys as Jay Berry was?
2. Draw a picture of the butterfly professor.
3. Illustrate to a classmate how the net contraption works.
4. Organize a grocery list of items you might purchase from Grandpa's store.

ANALYSIS:
1. Put together four statements that contrast the opinions of Daisy and Jay Berry toward animals.
2. Which three emotions did Jay Berry express in these chapters?
3. Compare how Daisy and Grandpa react to Jay Berry's first experiences with the monkeys.
4. In what parts of chapters 5 and 6 would you feel embarrassed if you were Jay Berry?

SYNTHESIS:
1. What if the animals lost from the circus had been lions? How would this have altered the story?
2. Create your own prophesy similar to Daisy's prediction that if Jay Berry didn't quit catching things a bolt of lightning would split him wide open.
3. Imagine you are Jay Berry and you have scared your family's prize goose away. How would you feel?
4. Create a cartoon which depicts some part of these chapters that has a message. Make it similar to an editorial cartoon.

EVALUATION:
1. What adjective would best describe the following characters: Jay Berry, papa, mama, Daisy, Grandpa, and the professor?
2. Why do you think Grandpa wanted to keep the monkey business a secret from grandma?
3. Determine what you think Jay Berry will really do with the money.
4. Decide whether this new attempt to catch the monkeys will work. Explain your reasoning.

Chapters 7 and 8

VOCABULARY:

maneuver	slithered
tantrum	pallet
trance	passel
hydrophobia	

KNOWLEDGE:

1. At what time of day did Jay Berry and Rowdy go to the hole with the net contraption?
2. Who did they see on their way?
3. What did Rowdy look like after Daisy's doctoring?
4. What is the hundred dollar monkey's name?

COMPREHENSION:

1. Why would Jay Berry leave the country and never come back if he had a little money and some groceries?
2. Describe how the monkeys overtook Rowdy.
3. Explain how papa relieved some of Jay Berry's fear of hydrophobia.
4. How did Grandpa figure that the hundred dollar monkey had a name?

APPLICATION:

1. Role play the chimpanzee and Jay Berry. Discuss what they might communicate if they could understand each other.
2. Read some other stories about life in the 1880s. Note the similarities.
3. Interview someone who works with the communication of animals.
4. Draw a portrait of the chimpanzee. Name him.

ANALYSIS:

1. Using a timer, write as many words as you can think of that describe Rowdy.
2. Research the characteristics of monkey behavior to help explain the squalling and jumping actions of the monkeys.
3. Examine Grandpa's reasoning about catching animals. Do you believe this?
4. Compare the fear of getting hydrophobia in the 1880s to what we might fear catching today.

SYNTHESIS:

1. Develop a new plan for Jay Berry and Rowdy to catch the monkeys.
2. What would have happened if Jay Berry had been able to get the two monkeys home?
3. What is the effect on Jay Berry when Daisy is always telling mama about his actions?
4. Communicate an idea using gestures and mime.

EVALUATION:

1. Summarize chapters 7 and 8 in your own words.
2. What would you have done at the beginning of the monkey attack?
3. Appraise Daisy's character. Why do you think she so enjoys nursing?
4. Jay Berry has a new approach to catching the monkeys. Predict if it will work.

Chapters 9 and 10

VOCABULARY:

moonshiner   fermenting

sly   buckboard

determination

KNOWLEDGE:
1. What did Jay Berry attract by calling for Jimbo?
2. What did Jay Berry lose this time while trying to catch the monkeys?
3. Recall how Jay Berry gets new britches.
4. Where does Grandpa think one can find all the answers?

COMPREHENSION:
1. Does Daisy have faith in Jay Berry's ability to catch the monkeys? Explain.
2. Why does Rowdy hesitate to go to the bottoms with Jay Berry?
3. How did Jay Berry and Rowdy get drunk?
4. Why did Rowdy growl and not let Daisy near him?

APPLICATION:
1. Write a brief outline sequencing what happened in chapters 9 and 10.
2. With a classmate, dramatize the scene where Jimbo offers Jay Berry sour mash.
3. Relate an instance where someone has done something once and is labeled.
4. Research in the library how wild animals are caught.

ANALYSIS:
1. Jay Berry felt embarrassed by calling Jimbo. Relate an incident where you have felt the same way.
2. Examine the actions of Jimbo when offering Jay Berry the sour mash. Compare them to human characteristics.
3. Calculate what Grandpa's next suggestion for the monkeys will be.

SYNTHESIS:
1. Create a five-panel cartoon showing: (1) Jay Berry and Rowdy going into the bottoms, (2) the monkeys around the sour mash barrel, (3) Jay Berry and Rowdy going home, (4) Daisy discovering Jay Berry, and (5) papa's reaction.
2. Develop an excuse for Jay Berry to give mama for losing his britches.
3. Daisy refers to Jay Berry as being a *drunk*. Analyze Jay Berry's reply "Just because I got drunk once, doesn't mean that I'm a drunk, does it?"
4. Wilson Rawls uses description to help readers *see* what he is writing about. Close your eyes and visualize while a classmate reads a paragraph from these chapters.

EVALUATION:
1. Judge how you think the monkeys feel after drinking the sour mash.
2. What is your conclusion concerning the intelligence of Jimbo?
3. Did Daisy have a good cure for Jay Berry? Why?
4. Why weren't papa and Grandpa angry about Jay Berry's getting drunk?

Chapters 11 and 12

VOCABULARY:
  codger
  witness
  covey
  column
  mercantile

KNOWLEDGE:
  1. What event took place on the way to Tahlequah that both scared Jay Berry and made him proud?
  2. Recall what mama told Jay Berry to do while he was away in Tahlequah.
  3. What did Grandpa and Jay Berry find in place of the coconuts?
  4. Daisy was not happy about losing her ribbons. What did Jay Berry have to do to appease her?

COMPREHENSION:
  1. Why did the students laugh in the library at Tahlequah?
  2. Describe the campus at Tahlequah.
  3. Why did Jay Berry call the coconuts *Monkeynuts*?
  4. Explain what happened to the coconuts.

APPLICATION:
  1. Research and report about the Cherokee Nation.
  2. Find Tahlequah on a map of today. List facts of size, colleges, or other points of interest.
  3. List what you might want at the mercantile store.
  4. What three logos would not appear in the town of Tahlequah at the time Jay Berry and Grandpa visited?

ANALYSIS:
  1. People learn from making mistakes. What three things has Jay Berry learned about catching monkeys?
  2. Write a short advertisement you might use at the mercantile store.
  3. Analyze the relationship of Grandpa and Jay Berry. How would you describe the influence Grandpa has on Jay Berry?
  4. Grandpa had always laughed at Jay Berry's misfortunes with the monkeys. Why didn't he laugh when the coconuts were traded?

SYNTHESIS:
  1. Draw a picture of Grandpa and Jay Berry entitled The Big Moment.
  2. How might the passing of time change things in Tahlequah? Make a list of the many, varied things you can think of that would be different.
  3. Write an imaginative dialogue between Jay Berry and the monkeys when they traded the coconuts for his britches.
  4. Contrast what the library looked like to Grandpa and Jay Berry to your library today.

EVALUATION:
1. Select three things in these chapters you found humorous. Share with classmates. Do we always agree on what is funny?
2. Grandpa states "You can't ever tell; might even be a highway come by here." How does he know?
3. Interpret the feelings of Jay Berry when he confronted the girl at the mercantile. Why was he uncomfortable?
4. Have you ever tried to catch something? How did you feel? How does Jay Berry feel at the end of chapter 12?

Chapters 13 and 14

VOCABULARY:
pulley
forge
legend
anvil
whippoorwill

KNOWLEDGE:
1. Who is Thor?
2. What is Jay Berry afraid might have happened to the monkeys during the storm?
3. What did Daisy find in her playhouse?
4. Why do fairies make a ring?

COMPREHENSION:
1. Interpret why Daisy laughed at Jay Berry's statement "We'll be lucky if we don't wake up dead in the morning anyway."
2. Papa believed Jay Berry would get his gun and pony. Explain how.
3. What is the music of the hills?
4. Express what papa's philosophy was on getting wishes.

APPLICATION:
1. Create a scene similar to Daisy and Jay Berry in the storm. Tell a brief story about it.
2. Interpret why Jay Berry gets so angry at Daisy and mama's kidding.
3. Read to the class a section in either chapter.
4. Make a wish.

ANALYSIS:
1. Distinguish between fact and opinion. Write three facts in chapter 13 and three opinions or fantasies.
2. Look into Daisy's story of Thor, the thunder god.
3. Research a legend.
4. Name the emotional tone at the beginning, middle, and end of chapter 14.

SYNTHESIS:
1. Imagine a perfect morning. What would it include?
2. Develop a plan of what you are going to do when you get a little older. Use your imagination.
3. What if there were no legends or wishes, only facts in the world? What would happen?
4. Briefly write Rowdy's wish for Jay Berry.

EVALUATION:
1. Daisy is always critical of Jay Berry. What does her action of going to him during the bad story mean to you?
2. Do you think Daisy would make a good storyteller?
3. Decide if you think Rowdy was making a wish in the fairy ring.
4. Do you believe Daisy's wish will come true? Why?
5. Why do you think Jay Berry changed his wish?

Chapters 15 and 16

VOCABULARY:
numb
gorilla
flabbergasted
moneypoke

KNOWLEDGE:
1. How many monkeys did Jay Berry rescue?
2. What is Jay Berry's explanation of why the monkeys bit him and Rowdy the first time?
3. Where was the circus performing when Jay Berry found the monkeys?
4. Who is Indian Tom?

COMPREHENSION:
1. Describe the river and baby duck scene.
2. Determine what Jay Berry means when he says to Daisy "If you don't stop feeding our apples to those monkeys, we're not going to have any apples left."
3. Why does Jay Berry make the trip to Grandpa's so quickly?
4. What happens to the monkeys?

APPLICATION:
1. Interpret Jay Berry's feelings when Jimbo laid his head on his shoulder.
2. Look into the difference between gorilla, monkey, and chimpanzee.
3. Imagine you are Jimbo. What "good-bye" would you tell Jay Berry?
4. Jay Berry and his family were poor yet they were happy and had things money cannot buy. List things that you need that cannot be bought.

ANALYSIS:
1. Contrast the reactions of mama and Daisy from when they first saw the monkeys to when the monkeys were in the corncrib.
2. List the human characteristics Jimbo displays in chapter 15.
3. Create a poster announcing Jimbo's return to the circus.
4. Describe the interior of the corncrib. Include Rowdy and the monkeys.

SYNTHESIS:
1. Create contrasting drawings of the monkeys at Jay Berry's first meeting and when Jay Berry found them after the storm in the bottoms.
2. How would you react if you had been mama and had seen Jay Berry walking to the house with Jimbo?
3. Do you think Jay Berry will really get a pony?
4. Write a brief statement telling what would be the biggest day of your life.

EVALUATION:
1. Why do you think the monkeys didn't bite Jay Berry or Rowdy?
2. Authors use vivid descriptions to help readers visualize the story. Give two examples. Are these passages effective?
3. Why do you think Grandpa gave Jay Berry a large bag of candy?
4. Jay Berry had worried, planned, and worked so hard to get the reward money. Why wasn't he happy when he got it?

Chapters 17 through 19

VOCABULARY:
fetlock
drummers
tendon
nickered
guilty
eerie

KNOWLEDGE:
1. Which pony did Jay Berry choose?
2. When did Jay Berry realize what Grandpa was trying to tell him?
3. What news in a letter made Jay Berry and Grandpa feel good?
4. What caused papa and Jay Berry to have a good laugh for the first time since Daisy and mama had gone to Oklahoma City?

COMPREHENSION:
1. Describe Jay Berry's feelings as he walked home with his paint pony.
2. Express what Jay Berry was feeling while mama and Daisy were in Oklahoma City.
3. How did Rowdy react to the train?
4. Discuss the feelings between Jay Berry and Daisy at the train station.

APPLICATION:

1. Interpret what Grandpa means by "But sometimes a fellow can want something so bad he will overlook things that are more important."
2. Translate the statement "It was so still you could have heard a dream walking."
3. List some things you believe Grandpa would wish for if he had the opportunity.
4. Demonstrate what Jimbo might have done if he had seen Daisy running through the clover.

ANALYSIS:

1. Analyze Grandpa's feeling when Jay Berry arrives with the money.
2. Contrast Jay Berry's walk home with his pony and his walk back to Grandpa's.
3. Jay Berry had never seen a train before. Write three things you have not seen before. Share with a classmate.
4. Pretend you had never seen a train before. What might your reaction have been?

SYNTHESIS:

1. Arrange the characters on a chart. List four characteristics of each.
2. Create a symbol that would show what basic things one needs in a lifetime.
3. Create a place and display of where Daisy's crutch should be placed.
4. Make a time capsule of things from *Summer of the Monkeys* using pictures and statements.

EVALUATION:

1. Why do you think Grandpa brought the crippled paint pony for Jay Berry to view?
2. Did you think that Daisy had wished for a pony and gun for Jay Berry while in the fairy ring?
3. Judge which section or event in this story you related to and enjoyed the most.
4. Should we all believe in the rare fairy ring?

Additional Activities

VISUAL ART:

1. Make a booklet of illustrations from your favorite events in the story. Label your illustrations.
2. Cut out pictures of monkeys and chimpanzees. Make a collage.
3. Create a class mural of prechosen events in *Summer of the Monkeys*.
4. Make scenery for one-act plays.
5. A group of three students can summarize the beginning, middle, and the end of each chapter. Each creates a crayon illustration of the chosen section. Apply a thin wash of black or blue tempera over the entire picture. Combine all to create a patchwork quilt that visually summarizes the book. Yarn and fabric may also be used.
6. Using an opaque projector, white shelf paper, and markers, design a filmstrip. A narrator for each illustration is needed as it moves through the projector. This technique is adaptable to action scenes such as those in chapters 4 and 9.

CREATIVE WRITING:

1. Write a one-act play from your favorite scenes.
2. Wilson Rawls uses figurative language to provide concreteness for the reader. Many examples are in the book. Create a page of similes and metaphors that are your favorites. Make up some of your own.
3. Videotape a news broadcast based on a favorite chapter using one or more of the following: interview Jay Berry; report the news; call-in opinion poll.
4. Think about the many lessons that Jay Berry learned in this story. Change his learning experiences into fables. State the moral in the final paragraph.
5. Write a script based on using local colloquialisms.
6. Write a story as told by Rowdy following Jay Berry through a typical day.

DRAMA:

1. Have a *Summer of the Monkeys* dress-up day. Students come as a character of their choice. They make homemade bread or churn their own butter.
2. Dramatize the student's creative writing one-act plays.
3. Experiment with storytelling as a student reads or tells excerpts from selected chapters. For example, in chapter 4 one student may narrate while students dressed as Jay Berry and the one hundred dollar monkey silently act out the more humorous scenes. Follow up with a professional storyteller.
4. Using the primary character's personality, retell one happening in his life in his own unique style. Keep in mind his speech patterns, what you perceive to be his manner of walking, sitting, gesturing, etc. Do it in the style of Will Rogers.
5. Role play a conversation between two of the characters.

SOCIAL STUDIES/SCIENCE:

1. Have students look up items in an old catalog or *National Geographic* to determine what the price of items during the time of *Summer of the Monkeys* and what they might want to purchase.
2. Have class members talk with grandparents or older friends about events and how things used to be. Discuss with class members.

3. Design a game with topographic landmarks starting with the bottom monkey tree and ending at the circus. Market your game.
4. Have students write a short essay selling the *Summer of the Monkeys*. Make an illustration to represent their favorite scene.
5. Brainstorm a list of activities that people did for fun in the 1880s.
6. Research the Cherokee alphabet. Write a note to a partner concerning your opinion of seal hunting or, perhaps, endangered species using the alphabet.
7. Write a letter to your local humane society to learn ways to aid animals. Share the information with your class.
8. Learn about research being done concerning communication with monkeys, dolphins, and whales. *Koko's Kitten*, by Francine Patterson (New York: Scholastic, 1985), relates new communication research.
9. Learn more about Will Rogers, the Oklahoma humorist. Find out why his style of humor was unique.
10. The Trail of Tears drama was centered near Tahlequah, Oklahoma. Find out how the Cherokee Nation began. Take notes and share your findings with your class.
11. Organize a Grandparent's Day. Interview your guests to find out about past historical events. Publish a class newspaper reporting the anecdotes and stories.
12. Research the land area comprising the Cherokee Nation. Using a U.S. map, mark off the involved area. Note the particular section where the farm was located as well as the area commonly referred to as "Cherokee Land."
13. Create a board game for Daisy that would reflect her belief in the old man of the mountains.
14. Construct an example of either a log or sod cabin. Compare the advantages and disadvantages of both.
15. Study the geography/topography of the Cherokee Nation.
16. Make a display of the different leaves from trees mentioned in the story. These may be either pictures or real.
17. Research animals that are being hunted to the point of extinction. Find out if there are prohibitions against the practice. Present the facts to your class. Take an opinion poll to see the group feeling concerning your report.
18. Research trees native to the Cherokee land. Collect leaves from your area.
19. Using seeds of wild flowers or grass from your area, plant them varying the conditions. One variation might involve planting half of the seeds in dirt and the rest in another medium such as a wet sponge. Compare the growth rates.

MUSIC:

1. Research mountain music and handcrafted mountain instruments. Invite an expert on such instruments such as dulcimers to your class for a demonstration and interview. Follow up by creating your own instrument.
2. Write a Jay Berry or Grandpa song based on a mountain melody. The lyrics could tell about an exciting incident in the story.

Bulletin Board

1. Discuss with students the management of journals which are accurate accounts of experiences and emotional reactions.

2. Elicit individual journal interpretations about past humorous experiences in each child's life period. Themes might include: (1) the funny thing that happened when I learned ... , and (2) the laugh was on me when....

3. Examples of student's writings are placed on large apples on the tree.

4. Jay Berry's account of the comic sour mash caper in chapter 9 is put on the large apple on the trunk as an example.

Readers Theatre*

CHAPTER 2

Cast: Grandpa Jay Berry

Jay Berry: "Grandpa, Rowdy treed a monkey!"

Grandpa: "Now let's do that all over again—only this time don't talk so loud."

Jay Berry: "You mean you want me to go back outside, Grandpa, and come in again?"

Grandpa: "No, no, you don't have to go back outside. Just say that all over again."

Jay Berry: "Rowdy treed a monkey."

Grandpa: "Are you sure it was a monkey?"

Jay Berry: "Sure as I need a haircut, Grandpa. It was a monkey all right. Papa thinks it was a pet monkey that belonged to a fisherman and it got away from him."

Grandpa: "No, I don't think it belonged to a fisherman. Is one monkey all Rowdy treed?"

Jay Berry: "That's all I saw, Grandpa, but I believe there was something else around there. I heard a lot of noises."

Grandpa: "Noises? What kind of noises?"

Jay Berry: "It sounded like cries and squeals, barks, and grunts, and everything else. It scared me into a running fit."

Grandpa: "I'm pretty sure those noises you heard were more monkeys. From what I understand, there were probably about thirty of them."

Jay Berry: "Thirty! Boy, that's a lot of monkeys, Grandpa. Are you sure?"

Grandpa: "I can't be positive, but I'd be willing to bet my last bucket of sorghum molasses on it."

Jay Berry: "Grandpa, do you know something about those monkeys?"

Grandpa: "Sure, I know something about those monkeys. That's what grandpas are for, isn't it? To know things for boys."

Jay Berry: "I guess so."

---

*Excerpts from *Summer of the Monkeys* by Wilson Rawls, copyright © 1976 by Wilson Rawls. Reprinted by permission of Doubleday, a division of Bantam, Doubleday, Dell Publishing Group, Inc.

CHAPTER 8

Cast: Daisy Jay Berry

Daisy: "Holy smokes, Jay Berry, what happened to you and Rowdy? Both of you look like you've been run through a briar patch."

Jay Berry: "Aw, Daisy, didn't anything happen to us. We just had a little fight with those monkeys and they bit us a few times. That's all."

Daisy: "A few times! It doesn't look like a few times to me. It looks like those monkeys just about ate you up this time. Jay Berry, I'm scared. I'm scared half to death."

Jay Berry: "Scared! What are you scared of? The monkeys didn't bite you."

Daisy: "I don't care, I'm scared just the same. We don't know anything about monkeys. For all we know, they may have hydrophobia."

Jay Berry: "Oh, no, you won't. You're not practicing any of that stuff on me. I'm not sick enough to go through that again."

Daisy: "Good morning! And how are my patients this fine morning?"

Jay Berry: "Aw Daisy, you didn't have to say that. You were here just five minutes ago."

Daisy: "I know, but that's the way nurses do it. Let's see now, I think I have just about everything I need right now."

Jay Berry: "Daisy, if you think I'm going to take all that stuff, you're crazy. Why, I'd be dead before the sun goes down."

Daisy: "Oh, I don't think you'll have to take all of it, Jay Berry, but I won't know just what medicine you'll need until I examine you."

How to Eat Fried Worms

by
Thomas Rockwell

How to Eat Fried Worms

by

Thomas Rockwell

Billy has always been willing to take a bet, but this one is his greatest challenge. He bets his two friends that he can eat fifteen worms. If he accomplishes this feat, he will win fifty dollars to purchase a minibike.

Billy must eat one worm each day for fifteen days. His friend Tom gives him support and will share the new minibike if Billy wins.

This funny adventure takes the reader through the gastronomic horror of eating each worm. Billy has elaborate garnishes for his worm dishes and prepares himself mentally for each worm feast.

When it becomes apparent that Billy might win, Joe and Alan scheme to keep Billy from eating those last few worms. The friends become involved in conflict over cheating. Desperate to win, Joe and Alan plan some nasty tricks as the final worm count approaches.

After the fear is gone concerning the physical effect of the worms on Billy, the family joins in to help him complete the bet.

Each new day and each new chapter presents challenges and adventures for all the boys and their families. Will Billy eat that final worm and ride that new minibike? This comical story will have you in doubt right down to the last chapter or bite!

Chapters 1 through 5

VOCABULARY:
>   duel
>   fricasseed
>   furtively
>   schemer

KNOWLEDGE:
1. List the names of the main characters.
2. Where did Billy's first worm come from?
3. How did Alan and Joe prepare the worm?
4. What did Billy use to cover the taste of the worm?

COMPREHENSION:
1. Describe Alan.
2. What is the meaning of "You're Chicken!"?
3. Demonstrate how Billy reacted to eating the night crawler.
4. Just suppose you were offered a bet to eat fifteen worms. How would you react?

APPLICATION:
1. What food do you especially dislike? Explain what is disagreeable about the food.
2. Make a classification of worm types.
3. Have you ever made a bet that was difficult? Share with your classmates.
4. What do you use on food that you would add if you were eating a worm?

ANALYSIS:
1. Survey your class for foods that are liked and disliked.
2. What part of chapters 1 through 5 did you find funny?
3. Evaluate what components of worm eating would be disagreeable or agreeable.
4. Inspect two worms. Note differences and similarities.

SYNTHESIS:
1. Make a commercial for your class advertising a box of worms. List ingredients, vitamins, etc.
2. Translate the thoughts of Billy while he was eating his first worm.
3. What if the worm had been an insect? Alter Billy's reaction.
4. Write an imaginative paragraph describing your reaction to a worm being served to you on a silver platter.

EVALUATION:
1. Why do you think Billy is always taking on challenging bets?
2. Will Billy eat all fifteen worms? Give reasons for your answer.
3. What do you think of this bet?
4. Would Billy's parents approve of this bet? Explain.

Chapters 5 through 12

VOCABULARY:

deracinate   apoplectically
indignant   chaff

KNOWLEDGE:
1. What is the main thing that bothers Billy about eating the worm?
2. How many worms has Billy eaten?
3. What does Tom suggest Billy think of while eating the worm?
4. Who are "The Plotters"?

COMPREHENSION:
1. Does Tom also eat a worm? Explain what happens.
2. What is it that Joe and Alan want Billy to feel when they talk about Joe's mother's reaction to the thought of him eating a worm?
3. Why does Billy want Tom to eat a worm too?
4. Why does Billy eat the worms in the barn?

APPLICATION:
1. Illustrate chapter 11.
2. Role play Alan, Joe, and Billy in the scene where Billy is eating the fifth worm.
3. Billy talks to himself in order to gather strength to eat the worm. Have you ever talked yourself into or out of doing something? Share the experience with your classmates.
4. Compare the different reactions to eating worms by a human and a fish. Why do they differ?

ANALYSIS:
1. Analyze how Tom felt when he was asked to eat a worm like Billy.
2. If Billy loses, he must come up with fifty dollars. Analyze how he would get the money.
3. Predict what Billy will say when he meets Tom again.
4. What do you think might be some food sources in the year 2500? Will worms be included?

SYNTHESIS:
1. Develop a worm recipe to share with your class.
2. Create a chant you would use if you had to eat a worm.
3. Collect pictures of worms. Construct a collage on a paper plate.
4. Write a poem about eating a worm.

EVALUATION:
1. Why do you think Tom calls the minibike "our minibike"? Is that fair?
2. Billy has eaten five worms. Will he continue?
3. Do you think the fact that Tom did not eat the worm will change his relationship with Billy?
4. Judge your feelings about Joe and Alan plotting. Are they wrong?

Chapters 13 through 20

VOCABULARY:
cleaver
antidote
discernible
virtuous
tentatively

KNOWLEDGE:
1. How many more worms must Billy eat?
2. List all the many, varied, and unusual worms you can find information about.
3. Who is to see that Billy eats worms ten and eleven?
4. Whom did Billy's mother want to call?

COMPREHENSION:
1. What causes Billy to feel better about his stomach pain and to be able to sleep?
2. Describe what happens to the ninth worm.
3. Explain why Billy was able to eat the sixth, seventh, and eighth worms so easily.
4. Explain why Joe and Alan cannot watch Billy eat worms ten and eleven.

APPLICATION:
1. Draw a cartoon strip showing Billy eating each worm.
2. Compare and contrast eels and worms. Make a list of similarities and differences.
3. Write a brief paragraph from a worm's viewpoint about being eaten by Billy.
4. Construct a clay model of one of Billy's worms.

ANALYSIS:
1. Analyze the "I think" in the sentence about Billy's stomach pain, "Oooo, there it goes again, I think."
2. What if all worms became extinct? Explain the effect.
3. Draw pictures which show the differences between three types of worms.
4. Find out why night crawlers are seen more in the evening than at other times.

SYNTHESIS:
1. Design a plan for Joe and Alan to have Billy give up the bet.
2. Predict how Billy will prepare worms ten and eleven.
3. Research what earthworms eat. Design a menu.
4. Create a new worm derived by taking characteristics of one or more worms and interchanging them. Illustrate your new worm.

EVALUATION:
1. Do you think Billy's mother will make him eat the worms? Why?
2. What is your opinion about the statement that if you are a liar and a cheat nothing you say is true. Justify your opinion.
3. Were Alan and Joe cheating in chapter 19? Explain.
4. Do you think it would be cheating if Billy made hash out of a worm? Justify your opinion.

Chapters 21 through 29

VOCABULARY:
envious
wrenched
pelted

KNOWLEDGE:
1. What is the name of the eleventh worm dish?
2. Who reminded Billy that he had not eaten the worm?
3. Why did the boys fight after Billy ate worm twelve?
4. Recall what Tom and Billy used to get Alan and Joe's attention while Billy ate the worm.

COMPREHENSION:
1. What is Joe's plan for winning the bet?
2. Describe Joe's father's reaction to trying to trick Billy.
3. Why did Tom want Billy to eat the worm where Joe and Alan would see him?
4. Explain why eating worm number twelve was more distasteful than the others.

APPLICATION:
1. Choose a recipe from a cookbook and substitute worms. Rewrite the recipe.
2. Relate Billy's parent's reaction to eating worms to your parent's. Would their reaction be the same?
3. Role play telling your parents that you are eating worms for a bet.
4. Write a brief summary of what has happened thus far in the story.

ANALYSIS:
1. Analyze the titles of chapters 23, 25, and 26.
2. Interpret illustrations you would make for these chapters to relate the action. List or draw them.
3. Prepare a short lesson to present to your classmates on the differences and similarities of two types of worms.
4. Make a survey of your classmates to see if Billy should give up the bet.

SYNTHESIS:
1. Create a title for a "worm cookbook."
2. Predict what chapter 30's title, "The Peace Treaty," will mean.
3. Write a dialogue for the boy's fight in chapter 24. Substitute descriptive words.
4. Imagine you are Billy. What are you feeling at the end of the fight?

EVALUATION:
1. Evaluate why Billy's mother would not allow his father to taste the worm dish.
2. What do you admire about Billy?
3. Are Joe, Alan, Billy, and Tom friends? Explain.
4. What are the qualities you want in a friend?

Chapters 30 through 40

VOCABULARY:

awestruck	defrauding
lassitude	stagnant
fulmar	cistern
dejectedly	cavorting

KNOWLEDGE:
1. Recall the ways Joe and Alan tried to stop Billy from eating the fifteen worms.
2. Who brought Billy the fifteenth worm?
3. What was the reason Mr. O'Hara gave for the boys to quit fighting?
4. Where was Alan going to put Joe on his final try to win the bet?

COMPREHENSION:
1. Explain why Billy had to go to his room.
2. Why was Joe at the store?
3. Explain the pun in Billy's statement "Do you think I could be the first person who's ever been hooked on worms?"
4. Summarize orally what happened in these chapters.

APPLICATION:
1. Have you ever learned to like something that at first seemed disgusting? Share your experience with classmates.
2. Plan a worm party. Draw party favors, games, refreshments, and invitations for your imaginary party.
3. Write a descriptive word for Alan, Joe, Tom, and Billy. Compare your words with classmates.
4. Write a newspaper advertisement selling this book.

ANALYSIS:
1. Analyze Mr. Forrester's feelings when he discovered Alan at the cistern.
2. Interpret chapter 38's title.
3. What lessons did the boys learn from the betting experience?
4. Think of some attributes of Billy's personality. Analyze what type of person he is.

SYNTHESIS:
1. Create an ending to the story where Billy loses the bet. Rewrite the epilogue.
2. Imagine worms are common in our diet. What would be some advantages?
3. Imagine you are Billy. Write a commercial advertising worms as a food. Present to the class.
4. Collect a bibliography of five research books on worms.

EVALUATION:
1. Do you believe that Billy will take on another bet? Explain your reasons.
2. Would you be friends with Joe and Alan after the bet? Explain.
3. Decide if worms may some day be a common part of the human diet.
4. What do you like best about this book? Why?

Additional Activities

VISUAL ART:
1. Create worms and garnishments from papier-mâché. Display on paper plates.
2. Make a mobile depicting the fifteen worms that Billy ate.
3. Create a worm candy bar wrapper. List ingredients and create an imaginative name for the candy bar.
4. Create a class cartoon mural. Cooperative teams are assigned a portion of the book to portray on poster board. Display in the library in the correct sequence.
5. Dye spaghetti and noodles. Using paper plates, have students make a worm dish with a title.

CREATIVE WRITING:
1. Write a creative story using the *How to Eat Fried Worms* plot but changing the worms to something imaginative.
2. Create a day-by-day newscast telling the main events of the book.
3. Have students write original titles for the book chapters.
4. Collect library books on the subject of worms and create a class display. Write a short paragraph on why you think worms are interesting.
5. Have students place all kinds of titles of books read and two sentences of why they enjoyed or disliked the book on large construction paper worms to place around the classroom.

DRAMA:
1. Choose a favorite scene from the book. Create a short drama for performance in the class.
2. Present a commercial for a worm product.
3. Choose a chapter in the book. Write a dialogue from the worm's viewpoint. Present to the class.
4. Make a worm puppet from an old sock. Present a play based on the book or dramatize the commercial from activity 2.

MUSIC:
1. Create a worm chant.
2. Research songs about worms.

SOCIAL STUDIES/SCIENCE:
1. Develop a rationale for the use of worms fifty years from now. Present to class.
2. Form teams to debate activity 1.
3. Discuss betting. Although Billy was in no physical danger from eating the worms, what could be some dangerous bets?
4. Make scrapbooks of different worm species. Have students share and display their work.
5. Research information on worm farming.
6. Form cooperative teams to research different types of worms in different topographical areas. Include environmental preference, poisonous species, and benefits to man. Present findings to class.
7. Compile a list of dishes containing insects or unusual edibles found at gourmet stores.
8. Observe worm behavior. Compile findings on a chart and report to class.

Bulletin Board

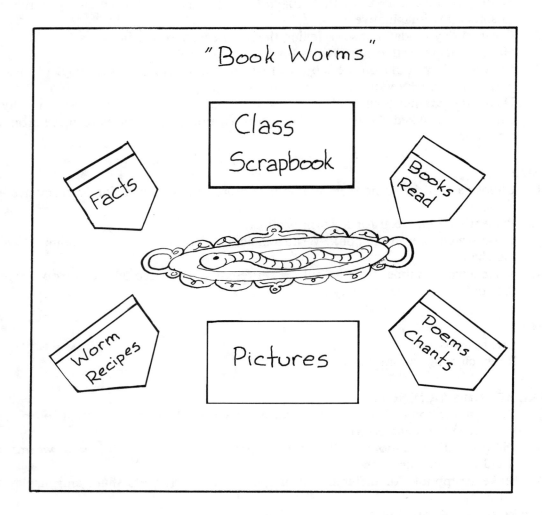

1. Students choose categories and write or construct contributions to the bulletin board pockets.

2. Contributions are shared. Favorites are placed in the class scrapbook.

Jelly Belly

by

Robert Kimmel Smith

Jelly Belly

by
Robert Kimmel Smith

Eleven-year-old Ned has a weight problem. He feels he is an outcast at school and at home. Students call him humiliating names that cause him to eat even more food. He is bullied by one of his classmates to the point he does not ride the bus to school, but rather walks each morning regardless of the weather. His best friend, Steve, seems to be the only person at school that supports and understands him. Steve accompanies Ned each morning on the walk to school. Ned's parents want to help him lose weight so they send him to a summer diet camp, away from a loving grandmother who indulges him with food and excuses.

At the camp, Ned joins his bunk mates in cheating on the eating rules. He is influenced by the camp bully, Richard, following his instructions even to the point of selling treats to other campers. As a result, Ned loses very little weight and returns home with his weight problem and guilt feelings.

Ned's brother is an excellent influence. He helps Ned realize what it takes to set a goal and achieve it. He also helps Ned to understand that the most important thing about achieving a goal is that one must want to do it themselves, not because others want it.

After Ned's father offers him a proposition of a trip to Disney World if he loses weight, Ned tackles the problem of getting his grandmother to cooperate and of losing thirty pounds.

Chapters 1 through 3

VOCABULARY:
>   brochure
>   criticize
>   contracts

KNOWLEDGE:
1.   Who is Ned's friend at school?
2.   What name bothers Ned more than any of the others?
3.   What is important to Ned that he cannot do?
4.   How many pounds overweight is Ned?

COMPREHENSION:
1.   Explain why Ned must eat differently than the rest of the family at mealtime.
2.   Why did Ned go to his room and cry?
3.   Express why Elizabeth hurts Ned so much.
4.   Describe Ned's family.

APPLICATION:
1.   Can you relate to Ned when he cries? What hurts you?
2.   Research studies on the dangers of being overweight.
3.   Have you ever called someone a name and later regretted it? Discuss.
4.   Relate the importance of Grandma to Ned's problem. What should she do?

ANALYSIS:
1.   Analyze the statement made by Steve in chapter 1 that makes him a true friend.
2.   Compare Ned's overweight problems to other problems one might be teased about.
3.   Find a newspaper advertisement for a weight loss program. What do they promise?
4.   Discover five high calorie foods.

SYNTHESIS:
1.   Design a list of names that people call one another and write what they mean.
2.   Write an advertisement for a diet camp to be printed in a magazine.
3.   Collect reasons for not being overweight.
4.   Design a chart that shows ideal weight ranges for a human from birth to age twenty.

EVALUATION:
1.   What do you think of Ned's parents' attitude concerning his diet?
2.   Is Ned's grandmother helping him? Explain.
3.   Predict what Camp Lean-Too will be like.
4.   Do you think it will be impossible for Ned to lose weight? Why?

Chapters 4 through 6

VOCABULARY:
> dietician
> reeducate
> urge

KNOWLEDGE:
1. What does Jamie want to be?
2. What was Ned doing about eating secretly?
3. Recall what was on the lunch menu the first day at camp.
4. Now recall why Ned ate his last breakfast at home so slowly.

COMPREHENSION:
1. Describe Jamie as seen by Ned.
2. Explain what Ned feels the camp will be like.
3. Describe the children at Camp Lean-Too.
4. What happened to Ned's cookies?

APPLICATION:
1. Do you have something you want, but not badly enough to really work hard at it? Share with a classmate.
2. Have you ever gone someplace new like Camp Lean-Too and were scared of what it would be like?
3. Write a brief paragraph about how you have persisted with something even though you felt fear.
4. Write a title for chapter 6.

ANALYSIS:
1. Describe the camp bunkhouse.
2. Compare the character of Richard to Ned's schoolmate, Phil Steinkraus.
3. Analyze Ned's attitude about Camp Lean-Too. Will this attitude help him lose weight while at the camp?
4. Compare your typical lunch to the first lunch at Camp Lean-Too. Calculate the differences in calories.

SYNTHESIS:
1. Prepare a list of your favorite vegetables. Assess which are high in calories.
2. Predict whether Gregg will discover Richard's corn chips in the tennis cans.
3. Research how the way you prepare foods determines calorie count.
4. Develop a statement that Ned might remember when he wants to eat something high in calories.

EVALUATION:
1. Was Grandma helping Ned when she gave him the box of cookies to keep? Why?
2. Is Richard being smart by hiding the corn chips in his tennis cans?
3. Evaluate Dr. Skinny's statement "forget about food."
4. Do you think the camp would be a help to someone overweight? Give reasons.

Chapters 7 through 9

VOCABULARY:
cooperative
suspicious
ridiculous

KNOWLEDGE:
1. What position did Ned like to play on the baseball team?
2. What is the doctor's name at the camp?
3. How many pounds is Ned overweight when he is weighed by the doctor?
4. What did the boys find in the kitchen?

COMPREHENSION:
1. Explain how the boys got the cheese sandwiches.
2. Describe Dr. Skinny.
3. Express the reactions of Hog and Max to the cheese sandwiches.
4. Describe how the letters from home made Ned feel.

APPLICATION:
1. Interpret your proper weight using your height and bone structure.
2. Research some old wives' tales concerning losing weight.
3. Write a report about a weight loss plan. Report to your classmates.
4. Prepare a crossword puzzle about diets.

ANALYSIS:
1. Analyze the meaning of Ned's statement "Talking with Dr. Skinny was like taking a test in school with someone giving you all the answers."
2. Compare the hamburger served at Camp Lean-Too to how you like them.
3. Compare and contrast the letters from home. How are they the same? How do they differ?
4. Analyze the effects of crash diets.

SYNTHESIS:
1. List three good habits and three bad habits you have or have experienced. Share how you have changed the bad habits.
2. Imagine you are at Camp Lean-Too. Write a short letter home.
3. Predict how you might have developed differently if you had been brought up in a different family.
4. Write a good riddle about Camp Lean-Too.

EVALUATION:
1. Should only persons worried about being overweight eat nutritious foods? Why?
2. Was Ned being honest in his first interview with Dr. Skinny?
3. Do you think Richard is a leader? Explain.
4. Estimate how much weight Richard will lose at Camp Lean-Too.

Chapters 10 through 12

VOCABULARY:
self-defeating
recommend
target

KNOWLEDGE:
1. How much weight has Ned lost in three weeks?
2. What is the best day and the worst day at camp?
3. What is Richard's nickname?
4. Where did Ned hide Grandma's cookies?

COMPREHENSION:
1. Describe the lunch on visitor's day.
2. How did Greg know that the boys had stashed food?
3. Restate how Dr. Skinny explains to Ned how the body uses food.

APPLICATION:
1. Illustrate chapter 11.
2. Give an example of an action that is self-defeating.
3. Write a title for chapter 10.
4. Draw a picture of what you would die for if you were at Camp Lean-Too.

ANALYSIS:
1. Analyze what Grandma means when she states "They take a good child and they make him a thief."
2. Survey your classmates. Record how many are happy or unhappy with their weight.
3. Analyze why not eating at all is unhealthy.
4. Ask your school cafeteria manager how he or she determines the school menus.

SYNTHESIS:
1. Construct a chart showing all the things that determine and affect your weight.
2. Imagine you are Ned after you had been at the interview with Dr. Skinny. How would you feel?
3. Create a camp song for Camp Lean-Too.
4. Design a graph showing Ned's weight loss.

EVALUATION:
1. How would you improve the program at Camp Lean-Too?
2. Compare Richard's parents to Ned's parents.
3. Why do you think Ned ate the whole can of cookies after his family left on visiting day?
4. Why do you think Ned felt bad after the visiting day?

Chapters 13 through 15

VOCABULARY:
orthodontist
innocent
enthusiasm
smuggle

KNOWLEDGE:
1. Why does Richard want to go into town?
2. Where did Max get the fifty dollars to take to town?
3. Where did Richard hide the stash of goodies?
4. Who took Richard to town?

COMPREHENSION:
1. Describe the plan to get into town.
2. Why was Richard looking for a dishonest man?
3. Who does Richard blame for being fat? Express his reasoning.
4. What happened to the boys' stash of goodies?

APPLICATION:
1. Keep a record of how many calories you consume in one week.
2. Role play Ned and Richard concerning Richard's plan to sell candy bars.
3. Exhibit pictures and charts showing facts about good nutrition.
4. Make a mobile illustrating what the boys bought in town to eat in secret.

ANALYSIS:
1. Calculate different calories in different foods. Rank them from high to low.
2. Classify your calculations into food groups.
3. Translate the Roman's practice of going to the vomitorium to a modern illness.
4. Research information on Robert Kimmel Smith.

SYNTHESIS:
1. Prepare a list of things you must do yourself. Others may tell you, but these things you must do yourself.
2. Compose a motto for Camp Lean-Too.
3. Design a different plan for getting Richard into town.
4. Propose a plan for your school to instruct students on good nutrition and physical fitness.

EVALUATION:
1. Give reasons why you think Ned always gives into Richard.
2. Predict how Richard's plan to sell candy bars to other campmates will work out.
3. Why do you think Richard has so much control over Ned and the other boys?
4. What do you think the reactions of the other camp members will be when they are offered the candy bars for a price?

Chapters 16 through 18

VOCABULARY:
circulate
moron
banquet
insignias

KNOWLEDGE:
1. What did Ned like about Richard?
2. Who spoke up for Ned?
3. How many pounds had the winner at the Camp Lean-Too banquet lost?
4. What did Grandma have waiting for Ned when he arrived home from camp?

COMPREHENSION:
1. Why couldn't Ned sleep?
2. Explain why Ned said the one lesson he learned is that there should not be any next time at Camp Lean-Too.
3. Summarize what the boys did after the awards dinner.
4. Describe what Grandma did when Ned returned home.

APPLICATION:
1. Name a food you would hate to do without.
2. Write a title for chapter 17.
3. Check the phone book and see how many diet camps are in your area.
4. Role play Max imitating Dr. Skinny.

ANALYSIS:
1. Analyze what Jamie means by the statement "You can resist anything except temptation."
2. Relate some of your friendships to that of Ned and Richard.
3. Make three constructive criticisms of Camp Lean-Too.
4. Pretend you are attending the banquet at Camp Lean-Too. How would you like the menu?

SYNTHESIS:
1. Predict what will happen to Ned's weight now that he is home.
2. Write a poem or riddle describing Richard.
3. Organize a debate on the best ways to lose weight.
4. Compose a five-page journal of the last week for Ned at Camp Lean-Too. Write one paragraph for each day, describing Ned's feelings.

EVALUATION:
1. Decide why Ned could not sell the candy bars.
2. Is Ned fortunate to have a brother like Jamie? Assess their relationship.
3. Tell why you think Ned's summer was just as terrible as he predicted.
4. Judge why some campmates had lost weight and avoided temptation and some had not.

Chapters 19 through 21

VOCABULARY:
    entitled
    annoyed
    backsliding

KNOWLEDGE:
1. How much weight did Ned gain on the first day home?
2. What did the big chocolate cake make Ned feel like?
3. When is Ned going to start eating less?
4. How many pounds must Ned lose in order to go to Disney World?

COMPREHENSION:
1. Describe the meal Grandma cooked for Ned's homecoming.
2. Explain the deal Dad makes with Ned if he loses weight.
3. Describe Mister Pangalos.
4. Express what became clear to Ned in the noisy lunchroom.

APPLICATION:
1. How would you have felt if you were Ned's dad watching Ned eat the first meal at home after camp?
2. How do you feel about the beginning of school? Write four adjectives.
3. Ned felt full of confidence and strength when he decided to diet. Relate a similar experience you have had when you have decided on doing something.
4. Calculate approximately how many calories were in Ned's lunch that Grandma packed.

ANALYSIS:
1. Compare Ned's feelings about the beginning of school and his feelings about attending Camp Lean-Too.
2. Contrast Camp Lean-Too to Camp Sha-Kah-Na-Kee.
3. Think of the main problem Ned must face in order to lose weight. Are there others?
4. Describe a goal you have accomplished that made you feel pride and relief.

SYNTHESIS:

1. Assemble a list of things that would go into a healthy lunch for Grandma to pack.
2. Compose a conversation for Ned to help him make Grandma understand his problem.
3. Prepare a telegram from Ned telling about his decision to diet and mean it!
4. Choose one of the main characters in *Jelly Belly* and write a short paragraph on why you liked or disliked them and were pleased or not pleased by their actions.

EVALUATION:

1. Why do you think Grandma packs so much food in Ned's lunchbox?
2. Do you think Ned will hurt Grandma in order to cut down on his eating?
3. Why do you think Libby had no trouble with Phil Steinkraus?
4. Evaluate your feelings for students like Phil Steinkraus. What do you feel for them? Can you be friends and help them change? Explain.

Chapters 22 through 24

VOCABULARY:

digital
resist
scheme
smirked

KNOWLEDGE:

1. How was Ned feeling as he prepared himself for talking with Grandma?
2. When is Jamie going to secretly practice running?
3. How did Grandma react when Ned ate cereal rather than her pancakes?
4. What did Ned accuse Grandma of making him into?

COMPREHENSION:

1. Explain why Jamie is worried about making the cross-country race.
2. Describe Grandma's argument for Ned being overweight.
3. Describe how the jogging made Ned feel after his argument with Grandma.
4. Identify how Ned reacts to Grandma's plan to cut down on baking and cooking starchy foods.

APPLICATION:

1. Interpret how Grandma was feeling during the conflict with Ned.
2. Invite a nutrition expert to your class to speak.
3. Make a list of five words that describe Ned in chapter 1 and another five words that describe him in chapter 24.
4. Interpret Jamie's statement "Runners don't beat other runners in races. They beat themselves."

ANALYSIS:
1. Compare the Ice Age to Grandma and Ned's relationship.
2. Compare Grandma's qualities as remembered by Ned to the qualities of someone you know.
3. Take away the love between Ned and Grandma. How would they have behaved?
4. Analyze what Grandma thinks makes the family feel good and happy.

SYNTHESIS:
1. Draw a picture of Grandma in chapter 23. Compare it to the illustration in chapter 2.
2. List the attributes of Jamie.
3. Create a week of healthy menus for your family.
4. Originate titles for these three chapters. Compare yours with classmates.

EVALUATION:
1. What effect will the jogging have on Ned?
2. Judge why Libby and Steve do not believe that Ned is really dieting. Do you believe him?
3. Do you think Jamie gave good advice about dealing with Grandma? Why?
4. Judge whether Grandma will really help Ned. What do you think will be in his lunch box the next day?

Chapters 25 through 29

VOCABULARY:
straightaway
squad
prodded

KNOWLEDGE:
1. How many pounds did Ned lose in one week?
2. How long did it take for Ned to get down to his ideal weight?
3. When was the hardest time for Ned?
4. What place did Jamie take in the six-mile cross-crounty race?

COMPREHENSION:
1. Which fact about dieting did Mom give Ned that was discouraging to him?
2. Describe some of Ned's actions that made him think he was getting weird.
3. Explain why Ned felt the family would not go to Disney World.
4. Explain how Dr. Brandt helped Ned make it after all.

APPLICATION:
1. Translate a goal you have set for yourself and made it!
2. Dramatize the bus scene with the confrontation with Phil Steinkraus.
3. Construct a chart with the headings: Place, Time, and Feelings. Place sentences describing details of *Jelly Belly* under the appropriate heading.
4. What characters grow and change in the book? Which ones stay the same?

ANALYSIS:

1. Calculate the calories in Ned's lunch prepared by Grandma.
2. Compare the calorie count to Grandma's lunch in chapter 21.
3. Analyze the meaning of "Skinniness is in the mind. Fatness is in the mouth."
4. Compare the feelings Ned was having in the doctor's office to those when he decided to diet in the noisy lunchroom.

SYNTHESIS:

1. Formulate a goal statement about attaining something that relates to the same plan as Ned's but not necessarily weight loss.
2. Write a short epilogue to *Jelly Belly*.
3. Plan a meeting between Ned and Richard. What would they say to the other at the meeting?
4. Design a computer game with graphics in which you have a goal of weight loss and choose items to eat or activities to do. Calorie count determines the winner, i.e., jogging knocks out so many calories, nutritious lunches, etc.

EVALUATION:

1. Evaluate the effect of the notes in Ned's lunch box to his attitude toward eating less.
2. Do you think that Grandma feels useful in Ned's eating less project? Why?
3. Assess the two obstacles Ned overcomes in this book. Discuss.
4. What do you think Richard, Hog, and Max will be doing during the next summer?
5. Do you think Ned will ever return to Camp Lean-Too?
6. Who, in your evaluation, is the hero of this book?

Additional Activities

VISUAL ART:

1. Divide the class into groups. Have students paint a mural of the main events of *Jelly Belly*.
2. Fold a large piece of paper into thirds and draw *before*, *in-between*, and *after* pictures dealing with *Jelly Belly*.
3. Do a mosaic using words and pictures from magazines related to the book.
4. Design a two-sided bookmark with one side showing Ned in chapter 1 and one side showing Ned in chapter 29.

CREATIVE WRITING:

1. Ask students to put themselves in the place of Ned. Write an essay about his feelings and attitudes. Videotape presentations.
2. Have students be literary critics of *Jelly Belly*. They should write responses to the following questions in complete sentences.

    1. Could the events in the book really happen? Why or why not?
    2. Is the dialogue in the book realistic?
    3. Are the illustrations good portrayals of the story?
    4. Did you learn anything from reading this book?

3. Have students cut out advertisements from magazines or newspapers concerning diet programs, then identify figures of speech such as similes, metaphors, or personification.

DRAMA:
1. Role play a dietician. Give a health speech on a particular diet you feel is effective.
2. Dramatize a commercial message to sell your diet.
3. Interview Ned exploring his needs, triumphs, and disappointments.

SOCIAL STUDIES/SCIENCE:
1. Have a health food party with students planning snack foods to be served.
2. Present a decision-making lesson. Have students write a personal growth goal and keep a journal on their progress.
3. Have students design a coupon book containing realistic personal growth goals. For example, keep a clean desk for one month, stick with a study schedule for one month, be on time to class. When a goal is accomplished, students receive a reward in a variety of ways, such as skipping a spelling test or playing a game.
4. Observe and research how many television shows and advertisements or magazine messages are related to diets. Record and report to the class.
5. Research diets of different countries. Report examples of good and poor diets.
6. Form debate teams to discuss the value of different diets.
7. Design personal diet counters from foods eaten during one week.
8. Have students research foods that were eaten in the 1880s. Report to the class why differences in diet occurred.
9. Research social attitudes concerning weight.
10. Research how the body utilizes calories.
11. Study different body traits. List some characteristics you have inherited from your family.
12. Research some causes for obesity in our country.
13. Research what diets will be in the future.

Bulletin Board

1. Students write individual goals and place them in the goal pocket.

2. As goals are attained, students check them off with colored pens and place them in the end results pocket.

3. Short paragraphs are written by the students on how these goals were attained. These paragraphs are attached to the attained goals.

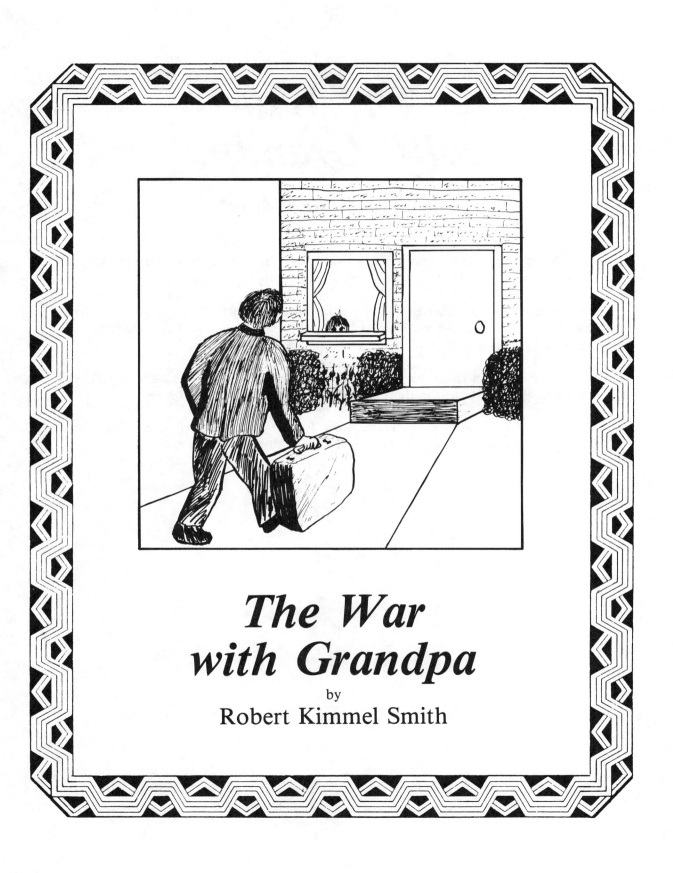

The War
with Grandpa

by
Robert Kimmel Smith

The War with Grandpa

by

Robert Kimmel Smith

This story is a humorous yet serious story about a young boy who lives with his parents and younger sister in a very comfortable home.

The best part of Peter Stoke's life is his absolutely perfect room. He never feels scared in it because he knows what every sound means. His stuff fits in perfectly. He can even find his way around in the dark.

Suddenly, Peter is told his grandfather is coming to live with them and he will need his room. Peter is pushed upstairs to a dingy, gross room he can't stand.

Peter declares war on his grandfather for the return of his room. The varied skirmishes and the ultimate lessons learned are both entertaining and wise.

Chapters 1 through 3

VOCABULARY:
  tacks
  pouts
  teeny-tiny
  pints

KNOWLEDGE:
  1. What was Mrs. Klein's theory on sentence structure?
  2. Where had Grandpa been living?
  3. What did Jennifer want Peter to include in his story?
  4. Explain why Grandpa Jack decided to move in with the Stoke family.
  5. Explain what initiated Peter's "war."

COMPREHENSION:
  1. How could Peter always tell Jennifer had a secret? Explain why she would usually tell them to Peter.
  2. Why didn't Peter ever get scared in his room? Cite some examples as well as his explanation for each.
  3. Relate how Mrs. Klein was responsible for the telling of this incident in the Stoke's home.
  4. Describe how Jennifer wanted herself to be perceived in this story.

APPLICATION:
  1. Create a shadow box showing the interior of Peter's room.
  2. Draw a picture of Jennifer illustrating why Peter thought she looked like a walking billboard.
  3. Create a monologue for Peter in which he describes the important things in his room, where they are located, etc. Be sure to convey their importance to him and his feelings regarding *his* room. Present this to the class.

ANALYSIS:
  1. Analyze the altering of Peter's opinion from his first learning of Grandpa Jack's arrival to that expressed at the end of this section. Explain.
  2. How might his emotions have been altered if Jennifer had never mentioned her secret?
  3. If you were involved in a situation similar to this, how would you approach it? Explain your position.

SYNTHESIS:
  1. Create a short dialogue where Peter might have expressed his concerns to his parents.
  2. Predict how Grandpa Jack might react if he knew about Peter's feelings.
  3. Imagine the possibility of a time warp where Peter, remembering his current feelings and concerns, suddenly found himself in his grandfather's position.

EVALUATION:

1. Hypothesize Grandpa Jack's feelings about being uprooted from his home and moving in with his children.
2. Compare and evaluate possible similarities in the attitudes of both grandfather and grandson—loss of identity, moving from a known locale, etc.
3. Read *The Mountain of Tears* by Paul David Mandel. It is the story of a Japanese boy who must deal with the problem of his aged mother. Compare the oriental attitude toward the elderly to that of the United States.

Chapters 4 through 6

VOCABULARY:

accountant	calculator
casino	birdbrain
slowpoke	maniac
plonking	gross
solemn	ledgers

KNOWLEDGE:

1. How did Peter express his opinion about dealing with bad news?
2. Explain the meaning of the term *tax time*.
3. What was one of the biggest mistruths Peter had ever uttered?
4. What does the term *slowpoke* mean?

COMPREHENSION:

1. Explain what Peter felt the responsibilities of an accountant entailed.
2. Why did his dad feel life wasn't always fair?
3. Describe why putting down his promise in "black and white" was important to Peter.
4. Considering Peter's point of view, what is a real asset to being a parent?
5. Did Peter offer a possible solution for all of the reasons Grandpa couldn't live on the top floor? Explain.

APPLICATION:

1. Using only a visual explanation, draw a picture showing the definition of the phrase *plonking away* at the piano keys.
2. Role play the telephone conversation between the parents and Grandpa Jack.
3. List the reasons Grandpa couldn't use the room on the top floor.
4. A rebus puzzle is one where a visual picture is used to illustrate a given word or phrase. Create a rebus for each of the following: slowpoke and birdbrain.

ANALYSIS:

1. Relate why you feel Peter titled chapter 4 "The Deadly Dinner."
2. Explain what you think Jenny meant by "I love him up to the sky and down to the ocean."

3. Do you feel Peter was proud of going into his room and crying like a maniac? Explain your opinion.

4. Analyzing the information given in this section of the book, which one of Peter's parents do you believe is Grandpa Jack's child?

SYNTHESIS:

1. Compose a poem entitled "Blue as the Sky" explaining Peter's feelings which created that phrase.

2. Create another poem with the same title as in activity 1, but this time using it as a positive base.

3. Design an invention to aid Grandpa in getting upstairs.

EVALUATION:

1. Judge why it didn't help Peter that his dad agreed with his opinion.

2. Discuss whether or not you felt the parents had considered the possibilities of Peter's reaction.

3. Judge who you feel is the most understanding of Peter at this point.

4. Interpret the validity of Peter's solemn promise. Debate if it would be feasible.

Chapters 7 through 9

VOCABULARY:

formica	weird
view	dinky
dim	boogeyman
terrified	idiot
hunky-dory	illustrated
emphysema	peapod
stooped	arthritis
pirouettes	depressed

KNOWLEDGE:

1. How many baseball cards does Peter have?

2. Why couldn't Grandpa Jack ever know how Peter felt?

3. What was the very last thing to be moved into the guest room?

4. How did the book about John Paul Jones help Peter?

5. Explain the reason Grandpa gave for developing arthritis.

COMPREHENSION:

1. How long has Peter been saving baseball cards?

2. Translate the phrase "mad as a wet hairnet."

3. Explain why Peter's room didn't feel as if it were his anymore.

4. Discuss the reasons why Peter felt his anger was justified.

APPLICATION:
1. Draw a picture showing Peter in the midst of moving to the third floor.
2. Report on the disease emphysema. Explain its causes and effect on people.
3. Draw a rebus showing Peter as a peapod and "springing up like a weed."
4. Sketch a head view of Grandpa showing him as he looked the last time Peter saw him as opposed to how he looks now.

ANALYSIS:
1. Analyze why Peter felt his new room was so scary.
2. Explain Peter's later rationalization for the strange noises.
3. Analyze the differences between the two children in being helpful.
4. What indication is given to show Grandpa might be as upset and unhappy as Peter?

SYNTHESIS:
1. Formulate a program where students can go to visit people in nursing or rest homes. Brainstorm different services or aids they could give the aged such as reading to them, talking with them, running errands, writing letters for them, etc. Try to set it up as an ongoing public service project.
2. Create an illustration showing your concept of Grandpa's feelings in his brand new life.
3. Translate the phrase "be still my heart."

EVALUATION:
1. Evaluate Peter's returning memories of his grandparents. How might they affect his current attitudes?
2. Interpret what constitutes a person as being *old*. Do you feel it strictly relates to age? Debate the varied class opinions.
3. Discuss how sadness or other strong emotions could alter one's life concepts.

Chapters 10 through 13

VOCABULARY:

mope	peppy
invading	fanatic
crinkly	wishy-washy
formation	tyranny
gorilla warfare	identity
revolutionary	

KNOWLEDGE:
1. Using the text, define the word *mope*.
2. What was Grandpa's synonym for *mope*?
3. Explain the correlation between a king and a grandfather.
4. What location heard the "shot heard around the world?"

COMPREHENSION:
1. Explain the phrase *scared silly*.
2. How did fictional characters like Zorro and Batman/Robin relate to this situation?
3. Recall the usage of the phrase *gorilla warfare*. How did the boys feel it should be used as a tactic in this war?
4. Which one of the three boys do you believe is more athletic? Using the book, cite the reason for your opinion.

APPLICATION:
1. Express by your choice of drawing or creative writing, one of Peter's memories of a happy time with Grandpa.
2. Draw a rebus showing both Steve and Billy's opinion of Peter's decision to remain quiet about losing his room.
3. Plant some seeds for the class. Follow their growth patterns during the school year. Discuss the various growth stages. When is the plant at its most sensitive point? When is it strongest?, etc.

ANALYSIS:
1. Compare the correlation Peter felt between the family taking his room to the book's description of the revolutionary war.
2. Arrange pictures of people in chronological order. This could either be from magazines or ones the students bring from home. Discuss the life stages and patterns from infancy to a senior citizen.
3. How had Grandpa's attitude changed since the last time he had been with the family? Discuss the possible reasons.

SYNTHESIS:
1. Have the students predict some changes that might occur before they have grown old. These might extend into the areas of medicine, automotives, electronics, etc. Write a short paragraph about their prediction.
2. Invent or design something new which would aid an elderly person. Brainstorm possible areas of need.
3. Create a dialogue between Grandpa and one of his friends in Florida in which he explains his attitude and feelings over the changes in his life.

EVALUATION:
1. Record various myths and stereotypes the students might have regarding senior citizens. Debate how these concepts might have evolved and the validity of them.
2. Discuss possible ways people can be educated about the needs of senior citizens.
3. Judge what you believe the feelings of Steve and Billy were toward Peter's problem. Were they helpful to him? Explain your position.

Chapters 14 through 18

VOCABULARY:

enemy   warrior
shivery   crinkling
declaration   ignore
digital   surrender
shielded   nonsense
kin

KNOWLEDGE:
1. Where did Peter put the note for Grandpa so he could be certain he found it?
2. What was Peter's special signature on his note?
3. Why didn't Grandpa say anything when he got the note?
4. Where did Peter go to write the note?
5. Recall what Peter said to his grandfather that showed he cared even though they were at war.
6. How much time did Peter give his grandfather?

COMPREHENSION:
1. Explain why Peter didn't want the note to be handwritten.
2. Describe how Peter acted when his grandfather came into his room so he wouldn't realize he had been awake.
3. Why was Peter so secretive when he was so positive he was right?
4. Explain why Grandpa saw similarities between Peter and his mother.

APPLICATION:
1. Role play the scene in Peter's room between him and Grandpa.
2. Research the beginning of several wars throughout history. Discover how *war was declared* in each instance and graph the results. Share your results.
3. Sketch Peter as the Secret Warrior.
4. Draw a picture of yourself as you think you will look as a senior citizen.

ANALYSIS:
1. Compare the usage of the words *gave* and *take* as well as *trick* and *war* as used by Peter and Grandpa.
2. In reality, what do you feel Peter wanted Grandpa to do considering he didn't want his parents to even know about the note? Discuss and compare different points of view.
3. Identify sections in the story that show the relationship between the three boys.

SYNTHESIS:
1. Design the front of a newspaper with the headline "WAR IS DECLARED!!!" Write an article describing this newest war.
2. Alter the situation by having Grandpa upset that he has to use Peter's room and not the one on the third floor.
3. Find an unusual way for Peter to express his feelings other than through the note.
4. Create a television interview involving the two sides in this war. Role play.

EVALUATION:
1. Judge which character you agree with at this point in the story. Support your opinion.
2. Interpreting the results of the research graph compiled in application activity 2, debate the ways wars are declared. Some examples might be the wars in Korea, Vietnam, and the Falkland Islands.
3. Determine what you think will happen to the relationship between Peter and his grandfather.
4. Predict the reaction of Peter's parents if, instead of Grandpa, they had discovered his letter.

Chapters 19 through 24

VOCABULARY:

fumble	truce
powwow	knobby
surrendering	gerbil
limpy	annoyed
monkeyshines	psychological
Machiavellian	meander
pish-tosh	dispute
grudge	obnoxious
encore	olfactory
feud	indubitably

KNOWLEDGE:
1. What does a flag of truce indicate?
2. What was Peter's second attack?
3. Which plan of attack did he reject?
4. Identify what really annoyed Peter.
5. How did Grandpa show Peter that war hurts?
6. What was the name of the fictional character Peter considered so very mean?

COMPREHENSION:
1. Explain the method Steve used to add words to his vocabulary.
2. Recall the alternate solutions Billy and Steve had for Grandpa's slippers.
3. Explain why Peter was having a difficult time keeping the war going.
4. What was Peter's interpretation of the means Jenny used to obtain her tutu? Explain how it altered from one person to another.
5. Explain why Peter didn't tell anyone about Grandpa slapping him.

APPLICATION:
1. Make a diorama about this section of the book.
2. Explain the portions of the story that could be best adapted to a book report.
3. Draw a caricature of Peter's concept of Jenny's performance for the family.
4. Research and report about Machiavelli.

ANALYSIS:
1. Research and explain the term *psychological warfare*.
2. Interpret Grandpa's feelings about the twists his life has taken.
3. Compare Grandpa's term *sneaky tricks* to Peter's *gorilla warfare*. Which term was more appropriate? Consider the term *monkeyshines*.
4. Analyze the similarities Peter saw between war and the game Risk.

SYNTHESIS:
1. Create a design for a flag of truce showing some of the special factors involved in this war.
2. Role play the scene between Grandpa and Peter where they are walking and talking about their problem.
3. Create a cartoon based on what you feel are the most important occurrences so far in the story.
4. Predict what will occur in the next section of the book.

EVALUATION:
1. Discuss Grandpa's views regarding war and the validity of his opinions.
2. Judge what Peter respected the most about his grandfather.
3. Interpret the change in Grandpa's attitude between breakfast and dinner.
4. Discuss the term *Machiavellian* and what it signifies in our language.
5. Evaluate why Grandpa's rebuttal was so surprising.

Chapters 25 through 30

VOCABULARY:

knapsack	diabolical	retrieved
repegging	asterisks	flounder
pizzazz	military	gravitational pull
leastways	prisoners of war	Damocles
tide		

KNOWLEDGE:

1. What did Grandpa consider prisoners of war?
2. Why didn't the Secret Warrior take the toolbox?
3. What did he end up taking from Grandpa's room?
4. Recall the reason Grandpa gave for the captured item being so important.

COMPREHENSION:

1. Describe how Grandpa showed he wasn't angry at Peter.
2. Explain Grandpa's attitude toward another attack by the Secret Warrior.
3. Tell why Peter made the decision he did about leaving a note.
4. How did Grandpa help Peter in front of Jenny?

APPLICATION:

1. Have the students bring newspaper or magazine articles telling about older people and their interests, activities, and achievements.
2. Take a class trip to visit a senior citizen center. Have them talk with the personnel about special needs of the elderly.
3. Look into the possibility of developing a foster grandparent program. The children could "adopt" an older person. They could make letters, cards, or pictures for them.

ANALYSIS:

1. Describe why Steve felt so good about Grandpa's retaliation.
2. Analyze why Grandpa's first attack was so very successful.
3. Relate the ongoing war to the change in Grandpa's attitude toward life.

SYNTHESIS:

1. Design a new game board using incidents from the story. If the incident was positive, such as the repairing of the rocker, have the player go ahead. Losing a turn might result from oversleeping the morning they went fishing.
2. Write an editorial about concerns families might have regarding care of the elderly.
3. Create a picture where the stars resemble asterisks.

EVALUATION:

1. Evaluate the change in Peter's attitude from Secret Warrior to grandson.
2. Discuss how you think Grandpa knew they were going to play Monopoly.
3. Have the students complete the following phrase with only one word, "Getting old is _____." Evaluate the answers. Are they negative or positive? Do you feel your opinion has changed because of this book?

Chapters 31 through 37

VOCABULARY:

panic
masterstroke
massive retaliation
conference
moonlighting
kerplunk

flip-flopped
indubitably
revenge
dingy
encouragement

KNOWLEDGE:
1. What was the first indication Peter had that his grandfather had "dropped the other shoe?"
2. How had Grandpa turned Peter's getting dressed into a treasure hunt.
3. What caused Peter to "flip-flop" to the breakfast table?
4. What did Peter and Grandpa agree that Peter had lost the war by?
5. How could Peter always tell it was grandfather coming up the stairs?
6. Show how Grandpa got serious.

COMPREHENSION:
1. How was Peter's mother involved with his shoelaces?
2. Why did Peter's relief at finding his knapsack in the right place turn sour?
3. Recall the incident where Grandpa was particularly devilish.
4. Explain why Peter waited almost a week to exact his revenge.

APPLICATION:
1. Role play the scene between Peter and Grandpa when he comes for his missing teeth.
2. List all the different things grandfather managed to do to Peter that morning.
3. Make a sign for your bedroom door showing that the room belongs to you.

ANALYSIS:
1. Explain how the notes grandfather left showed he really cared for Peter and only wanted to inconvenience him.
2. Analyze why Peter finally agreed with Billy that he really was chicken.
3. Relate how Mrs. Klein showed special understanding about Peter's story.

SYNTHESIS:
1. Create a drawing of Peter as he looked on the day of massive retaliation.
2. Design a code or language with your friends to replace key words from your school day. Examples might be lunch, recess, books, pencil, paper, and homework.
3. Draw a simple blueprint of the changes Grandpa was going to make in the basement.

EVALUATION:
1. Discuss the lessons each learned about respect for others and their dignity.
2. Evaluate what Peter perceived as being the hardest part of writing this story to other situations.
3. Decide why the ending of the story made him so sad.

Additional Activities

ART:

1. Make something to give to people in a nursing or rest home such as place mats, greeting cards, table decorations, etc. They can be for a particular holiday or just an expression of caring.
2. Have each child draw a face of a person. Either you reproduce them on the copier or have the children duplicate them until each has at least three. Leave the first one alone and age the others by adding frowns, lines, wrinkles, etc., producing the same face at varied stages of life—young, midlife, and old age.
3. Create a comic strip illustrating your favorite chapter in the book.
4. Have the students draw a picture of themselves as a senior citizen.

DRAMA:

1. Have students decide on a character in the story and create an appropriate costume. Then have them choose a scene, pose it, and a snapshot taken to be later identified or captioned.
2. If you have access to a stage and curtains, another variation on activity 1 would be to have the students act out living pictures. They begin the scene in a *frozen* position. Complete the scene and end up in a similarly *still* pose.
3. Role play the interaction of family relationships. Assign students to roles of parents, grandparents, children, etc. Either present them with given situations or have them create their own. Variations might include time changes (either past or future) or, after acting out a situation, having them reverse roles.

CREATIVE WRITING:

1. Encourage an Adopt-a-Grandparent program. Make contact with a nursing home, etc., and set up a pen pal correspondence between the residents and the students.
2. Write a treaty between Peter and Grandpa. Include the provisions they have agreed on.
3. Create a newspaper editorial regarding the concerns and care of older people in our society.
4. The story is from Peter's perspective. Have Grandpa write a letter to a friend in Florida explaining what's happening from his viewpoint.

MUSIC:

1. Take a song from the 1920 era such as "If You Knew Susie Like I Know Susie." Change the lyrics to express either Peter's feeling toward his grandfather or vice versa.
2. Reverse activity 1 by either choosing a current popular song or create a rap.
3. Learn a collection of both oldies and current hits. Take a choral to various rest homes and perform.
4. Learn or compare different dances from the 1920s and the 1980s. Some choices might include the Charleston, black bottom, moon walk, and modified break dancing.

SCIENCE:
1. In the classroom study the life cycle of different things such as caterpillars, seeds, tadpoles, etc. Have the students record and discuss the differences at each growth stage.
2. Research diseases commonly associated with aging such as arthritis, vision/hearing loss, osteoporosis, and Alzheimers. Survey as many senior citizens as possible, recording which ones are affected by any of the above. Chart your results and, from the basis of your data, infer the prevalence of each.

SOCIAL STUDIES:
1. Have the student either use the birthdate of the person they interviewed or a famous older person to create a time line from their birth to the present. This could record personal data, historical occurrences, scientific breakthroughs, or a combination of the above.
2. Research attitudes and care for the elderly in various cultures throughout the world. Possible choices designed to show different attitudes and customs might include those of Japan, China, Soviet Union, Sweden, and the Eskimos. Compare these practices to those of United States, Canada, and Great Britain.
3. Another approach might be the evolvement of care for the elderly through the years.
4. Prepare an oral history of your town, area, or state. This could either be of a general nature or take a specific event and interview people regarding their recollections of it.
5. Recreate your family tree, using the chart at the end of this section.
6. Many equate superior achievement with youth. Research several outstanding individuals who were noted for their accomplishments after the age of 60.

George Burns	Gregor Mendel
Pablo Casals	Grandma Moses
Maurice Chevalier	Carl Sandburg
Jacques Cousteau	George Bernard Shaw
Winston Churchill	Albert Schweitzer
Salvador Dali	Mother Theresa
Benjamin Franklin	Leo Tolstoy
Robert Frost	Queen Victoria
Golda Meir	Frank Lloyd Wright

FAMILY TREE

Paternal
Great-Grandparents

Maternal
Great-Grandparents

_____ and _____

_____ and _____

_____ and _____

_____ and _____

Grandparents

_____   _____

_____   _____

Father   Mother

_____   _____

ME

_____

Brothers and Sisters

Bulletin Board

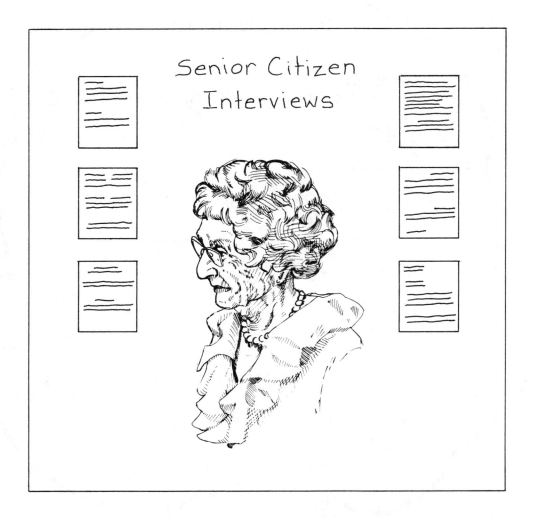

1. Have the students interview a senior citizen who is either a relative, family friend, or from a nursing home.

2. Possible questions should be discussed by the class establishing general guidelines.

3. The use of a tape recorder might be advisable so the student could take their time reviewing the information as well as eliminating time writing down the answers.

4. If possible, an added interest would be including either a picture of the person in their younger years, a photo taken at the time of the interview, or both.

5. Have the entire class share and compare their feelings.

Appendix:
Poetry Formulas

Some of the activities in this book call for the use of poems in the cinquain, diamante and haiku forms. This appendix provides the formula for each of these forms.

Cinquain

<u>Example:</u>

Happiness
Friendship, harmony
Companion comes near
Lively, enthusiastic, glowing, warm
Joy

Line one	Title
Line two	Two words describing title
Line three	Three words expressing action about the title
Line four	Four words expressing feelings about the title
Line five	One word renaming title

Diamante

<u>Example:</u>

Rejection
Lonely, unhappy
Stealing, crying, suffering
Confusion, despair, laughter, friendship
Creating, achieving, sharing
Joyful, loving
Acceptance

Line one	Noun (title)
Line two	Two adjectives describing title
Line three	Three present participles relating to the title
Line four	Four nouns (the first two nouns relate to the title, the last two, to its opposite)
Line five	Three present participles relating to the opposite of the title
Line six	Two adjectives describing the title's opposite
Line seven	Noun (opposite of title)

Haiku

<u>Example:</u>

Dove and persimmon
A misty, fleeting, mirage
Through the slender elms.

Line one	Five syllables
Line two	Seven syllables
Line three	Five syllables